CW00766470

OH WHAT FUN IT IS... U.T.B.

First published in paperback in 2013
by Sixth Element Publishing
Arthur Robinson House
13-14 The Green
Billingham TS23 1EU
Tel: 01642 360253

© Hal Gate 2013

ISBN 978-1-908299-50-5

British Library Cataloguing in Publication Data. A catalogue record for this book
is available from the British Library.

All rights reserved. No part of this publication may be reproduced, stored
in a retrieval system or transmitted, in any form or by any means, electronic,
mechanical, photocopying, recording and/or otherwise without the prior written
permission of the publishers. This book may not be lent, resold, hired out or
disposed of by way of trade in any form, binding or cover other than in which it
is published without the prior written consent of the publishers.

Hal Gate asserts the moral right to be identified as the author of this work.

Printed in Great Britain.

www.6epublishing.net

OH WHAT FUN IT IS... U.T.B.

HAL GATE

6e

www.6epublishing.net

FOREWORD

Football supporters are a special type of people but I've always found away fans to be a breed of their own. After all, it takes a specific type to want to spend long hours travelling to and from far ends of the country to support their local football team. And yet the backing they give their team on their travels can and often does make all the difference. Fortunately, Middlesbrough have always been particularly fortunate in that regard, attracting impressive followings to the far reaches of the country. That's why I'm delighted to have been given an opportunity to write the foreword for this book.

As a raw 18-year-old, I made my first team debut for Willie Maddren's Boro as a substitute for Don O'Riordan in an away game at Crystal Palace in March 1986. The record books show that there were fewer than 5,000 in Selhurst Park and yet my memory recalls a great following of Boro fans. Throughout the many incredible ups and downs of the years that followed, the core of that support remained, throughout liquidations, relegations, promotions, cup finals and the incredible experience of European football. The final game of my career came as a late substitute in Boro's final Premier League game before the 2006 UEFA Cup final, a memorable day that saw 10 of the club's Academy products start a game at Fulham. Once again, the Boro following was impressive, loud and proud and gave me a rousing send-off that will always live with me.

But travelling to away games to support your local team isn't just about football, as much as us players might have sometimes assumed. As this excellent book makes clear, it's about camaraderie, adventure and laughter, all usually washed down with a few beers too many! No doubt it's also mixed in with a massive amount of determination and sheer bloody mindedness when the results aren't going your way, but that's what makes the away fan such a special breed.

A sincere and heartfelt thank you to the author for contributing all of his profits from this book towards the Finlay Cooper Fund. When my wife Julie and I lost Fin shortly before his second birthday, we knew he would never be forgotten but this amazing fund has ensured his name lives on in a way that we could never have imagined. Thanks to the fund's wonderful trustees and so many big-hearted people, thousands of pounds continue to flood in for children's causes, most of them on Teesside.

Enjoy the book and Up the Boro!
Colin Cooper

CONTENTS

ACKNOWLEDGMENTS AND THANK YOU TO...

Ted, Chris an' Maca for showing me the way, Dave Brown, Ruth, Mac, Carter, Emily. Ronkey-Jonkey (the Beechwood and Easterside smilers), The Welshman, Posh, Lee D and Lee T, Tony 'The Fox', Craig, Dave 'The Cleaner', Jamie, Rob, Dom, Smart Mart, Sylvia, Sue Gardener, Harry Pearson, Colin Cooper, Arthur Miles (amazing photos), Andy D, Mike, WH Smith PLC and Gillie and Graeme at Sixth Element.

And lastly to the 'Great Anonerimus' who either willingly or unwittingly contributed through your stories and actions without which there would be no book.

All statistics for games taken from the official web sites of the home team.

INTRODUCTION

This was a simple idea. If you ever talk to another Boro supporter about going to the match, they normally tell you honestly what they thought of it. What would be even more important to them though, would be to tell you why they didn't go! Then tell you what they thought of it.

But talk to them about an away match? The first thing they will say is, "Eeee, I remember when we went to…" and off it goes. They will tell you about the game, the pitch, the ground, the team, the manager, the weather, the price of the pies, the beer and usually the state of the town they visited. But that is only half the story. There's the getting the tickets, the travel down, the digs (if an over-nighter is in order) and then there's the travel back… and so it goes on.

Everyone has a story about going to an away match. They may go every week or only once in a lifetime to Wembley. This then is a collection of conversations, observations, emails, texts and even a letter (if you remember them) I have had from Boro supporters across the country. Because this is a collection of their stories, it would not be right to take credit or make profit from other people's memories or opinions. Also I found that if you told people that their stories would be credited to 'Anonerimus', they tended to be more forthcoming in the detail. Telling them it was for charity kind of dissolved any guilt they had and helped make 'a bad thing good'.

As a lot of these experiences were told to me verbally (usually after a small amount of alcohol had been drunk) and because people tend not to write how they speak via email,

I found it hard to write them down other than in what can only be described as Teesside. The thing about our accent is that it's not 'true' to all areas. Redcar, Eston, Normanby, Flatts Lane and Lazenby all retain a Yorkshire twang that South Bank and Grangetown who are right in the middle of these estates just don't have… we're all the same but a little bit different. How many times when you hear someone on telly from our area, do you say, "Now that's a proper Boro accent, that like", only to find they are from Stockton or Billingham? It's very hard to pin down what area people are from. So I have tried to keep this difference in the quotes, yet make it so the reader gets a flavour of the speed and pattern we Teessiders tell a story. We also love what I call 'a pause for a punch line'. When someone tells you something, we like to finish it with a pause, then the 'last line' is normally funny or self-deprecating in some way; this is because if you don't, the other person will do it for you. We have an uncanny knack of bringing people back down to earth. I have also kept it as clean as possible without losing a little sauce or colour to flavour the dish so to speak. As a kid going to school in South Bank, the 'f' word was used almost as punctuation; this was to let you know the next word in the sentence was really important. That brings me to one last thing. Yes, shock horror, football supporters still swear at the match.

CHAPTER 1:
THE AWAY FAN

The Boro boys are
in town...

"I support Middlesbrough. When people ask me why, I say: because I'm a glory-seeker."
Harry Pearson, The Far Corner

What makes a perfectly sane person from Middlesbrough want to leave his nice warm cosy bed at stupid o'clock in the morning in the middle of February, cram himself onto a coach, train or, if he can find four other like-minded individuals, into a car. Then, travel the full length of the country either starving themselves or testing their nerve in an excruciatingly painful game of 'bladder control chicken' just to shorten the journey time, only to emerge at the other end into a car park or train station like rubber-legged Bambies blinking at the daylight. They are then herded like cattle or prisoners of war to their final destination, usually a cow shed in the middle of some waste ground. All this just to sit in the freezing cold for up to another four hours. Then repeat the process all over again on the return trip home. Well, the answer is… a 0-0 draw with Brighton Hove Albion… result.

The away fan has always been an enigma to the public, to

other supporters and even to the clubs themselves. The one same question is always asked by all home supporters as they look across to the opposite side of the ground: "Why?" And that question is at the very heart of this book.

Unless you are a supporter of one of the top six teams in the country or a Premiership side away to a small club in the cup, why would you follow your team all the way to another part of the country? Statistically, the home side holds the advantage and you stand less chance of seeing your team score let alone actually win. And that's the whole point of going to see them, isn't it?

So you can understand the Middlesbrough season ticket holder pondering this very question, as he sits looking across to the small group of lumpy-shaped Cheltenham fans. All huddled together more for warmth than safety. Why? Why come all the way from a lovely place like that to a hole like this only to see ya team get beat? See even Boro fans go to a home game thinking we have at the very least some chance of a win.

The thing is, people from Middlesbrough ask the same question to people from out of town when they come here to live. We ask them questions like, "What, you came here out of choice, not coz of work?" or "Do you have relatives here then?" or "Is there a history of bronchial diseases in the family, like?" and my personal favourite, "Why would you chose to come and live somewhere like Middlesbrough? Newcastle's only down the road, ya know". We are proud of our area but not so sure why. Being from Middlesbrough, it's as if we are born with a 'backs against the wall' mentality and I believe that shows through in our support for the club.

We all know football is a tribal thing. The identity of a

town or city is synonymous with its football team even across Europe. So much so that the success of a team can change the image of the area it hails from. Just ask Steve Gibson. He's been banging on about it for over 20 years. We also know if a town is prosperous and people have money in their pocket, they are more likely to go to the match. Good gates inevitably mean a healthier club and that attracts better players and better results follow. We as Boro fans know it works in reverse – that if the club has cash pumped into it and pays for better players, better results follow and the gates then increase. It's a positive for the whole town and its image either way. You see this time and again with teams like Man City or newly promoted teams. When things were going well, we all got more involved and the away travelling support was unbelievable.

That's what people take with them when they go to away games. They are a non-elected voluntary representation of your team's support. Because of this I believe they are also a true reflection of your home town. Even the words 'home town' to us Boro supporters can only mean one thing. But think of all them Manchester, Liverpool and Chelsea fans who align themselves to a team. Not through place of birth but just through choice. I would like to know if they carry the same pride or passion for their team as we do? There is no doubt they do support their club, some spending thousands to follow them in all competitions across Europe. But do they support their town if the people who live in a place define its identity? For us, the Middlesbrough playing on the pitch is almost an extension of ourselves. 'We' win and 'We' lose together. We are Middlesbrough.

As a Boro supporter when you're getting beat by Man U, nothing gives you more pride than to see a lad from Darlo come on and kick Christiano Ronaldo into row Z. I can think of nothing better for any professional footballer (worth his salt) than playing for his home team. That's what makes supporters from clubs like ours special. Given a choice, not many people with no connections to the area would choose Middlesbrough FC as their team. Can you imagine any teen girl living in Chelsea removing her picture of Frank Lampard and having a 1987 poster of a mud-covered Tony Mowbray on their wall? Actually when it comes down to it, I can't think of anyone doing that apart from, say, his mam.

Firstly, away fans look no different, talk no different and at first glance are no more passionate about their club than any other fan. But what makes them different is the extremes they will go to to fulfil their own personal goal. There are lots of different types of away fans and they do it for a number of different reasons.

Some arrive in the beast's belly of the away ground decked in total red and white, from their bobble hat to the XXXL replica kit worn on the outside of their coat. Others, a simple single coloured scarf. Some more cautious veteran supporters may wear no colours at all except for a small pin badge, while others dress up in full fancy dress from chemical warfare suits to a festive Santa outfit whether it's Christmas or not. To some it's a day out on the piss with the lads and away from the wife an' kids. Some, a chance to spend quality father-son time. Others just part of their membership to the supporters club and an extension of their commitment shown in a annual season ticket purchase. It's a family thing, a tradition passed down generation to generation, or even the simple unnatural train spotter's obsession with collecting every football programme ever associated with Middlesbrough Football Club.

Whatever the force behind it, the away fan stands tall in the league table of football supporters. The less successful the club, the higher the accolade for following your team round the country no matter how sh*t they are.

Whatever the reason, it can show the best and the worst of a town and its people. You can make friends that will last forever or meet people you just nod to in Tesco, an' when the wife says, "Who's that?" you say. "Just a lad that goes to the match," an' she will accept it without any further question as if it's a secret underground society she wants nothing to do with. But you can find that normal people behave very different away from home, like kids on a school trip to France or Flamingo Land.

So in short, I honestly have no idea why we do it. But the one thing that is true is that football as a game would be far less of an occasion if we didn't. Away fans can make the game or the atmosphere of the ground change in a single breath. Managers always come out and say things like, "I thought our fans were superb tonight," or "It was like a home game; they never stopped singing," and they sometimes repay the devotion as well with, "Our fans have come such a long way, we just wanted to give them something to smile about on the way home."

Just as a big home crowd has its effect on players, a good away support can take the edge off an intimidating fixture and that can make a difference to a result. So if you support your club and know that somehow you could positively affect the outcome of a game, why wouldn't you follow your club round the country, no matter how sh*t they are?

Anonerimus

Liverpool v Middlesbrough,
Premier League, 23rd August 2008
Score 2-1, Attendance 43,168

" We had a night out in Liverpool before the match an' we are in Walkabout. After a few we decided to move on, so en mass we all trot off to the bogs. We take up just about all the stalls and urinals available having a bit of banter as we go.

When we all start to push out the door, this little fella sat on a high stool in the corner goes, "Hay lads, would you like some scented soap to wash with?" We all look around, he's obviously trying to embarrass us, or just being clever that none of us have even thought about 'wash after you go'. Then the Boy Younger has a go back, "Nor, ya all right mate, we're from the Boro, we don't p*ss on our hands like you dirty Scousers. Cheers though, oh an' good luck in prison."

And they say people from Liverpool are quick. **"**

You'll never walk alone, Ayresome style.

Anonerimus

Middlesbrough v Man City,
Premier League, 11th May 2008
Score 8-1, Attendance 27,613

"Man City at home, last match of the season, sat in the Wetherspoon's about 11.30am. In walks a handful of City fans followed by four dressed as 6ft odd bright yellow bananas, proper full on big bloody bananas with just yellow Lycra arms an' legs sticking out of the sides. Most of the Boro fans just stand as if it's normal on a match day here in Middlesbrough.

We are all looking in silent admiration smiling at each other nodding, when in comes three Police Officers in yellow high viz jackets topped off with their traditional Bobby's helmets. One of the City fans turns round to look and quick as ya like shouts out, "Aye aye, here comes the rest of a bad bunch."

We all fall about laughing then a Boro fan shouts out, "Yea but you'll be the ones getting skinned today, lads", an' he was spot on as well. **"**

Everywhere we go.

Anonerimus

Blackpool v Middlesbrough,
Premier League, 18th September 2012
Score 4-1, Attendance 12,746

" Blackpool, a year ago, it was raining that hard we were sure they would call off the game. As we huddled in a packed pub doorway, I looked at the police all safe an' warm in their mini bus type vans. I thought if any trouble comes there's no way they are getting out to help us here.

A few minutes later, three Boro fans come jogging round the corner with these big traffic cones on their heads trying to keep the rain off. They looked like they had come in sh*t Mexican fancy dress. As they jogged alongside the police vans, the coppers switched on a quick burst of their lights and sirens. Well, these lads set off full pelt like scalded cats sprinting down the rain-soaked road. Did the West Lancashire police force chase down such wanton vandalism and misuse of the highway commission's property? No, they just sat in their van and chuckled to each other. Old fashioned policing can go a long way. **"**

For Virpi and the growing Boro global army, every home game is an away game.

Anonerimus

WBA v Middlesbrough,
FA Cup 2nd Leg, 22nd February 2007
Score 1-1 (4-5 on pen), Attendance 24,925

"
My brother's been seeing this lass for about a year and he's starting to get serious about her; getting all 'lovey-dovey', spending almost every weekend at her's. But he wanted to go to the cup match 2nd leg away.

"Bring her with ya," I said. "Call it a test. If she's up for it an' if she has a good time, ya know she's the one like."

So we go down on the coach, have a few on the way, an' a few in the ground. We win! An' then have a few on the way back. All this time she's been a little smasher. She's at the front of the coach with our brother but turned backwards, sat on her knees facing the rest of the bus singing her heart out, having a great time. Then from the back of the bus comes from one of the lads the obvious chant, "Get ya t*ts out for the lads." Then it really starts as nearly the full coach shouts, "Get ya t*ts out, get ya t*ts out, get ya t*ts out for the lads..."

So she shakes her head as if to say no... but then quick as a flash lifts her Boro top, bra an' all, over her head a la Ravanelli style and waggles her norkes at the whole coach... quality.

He ended up marrying her the next year. They live in Flatts Lane now and have two kids... ha ha ha love's young dream.**"**

What am I doing here?

11

Anonerimus

Nott Forest v Middlesbrough,
Premier League, 20th March 1999
Score 1-2, Attendance 21,468

"Going to one away game, we had to pick a lad up from site who was working the morning. So we are running late coz of him an' we bundle him into the back of the works van in all his worky gear, hi-viz, hard hat, the lot. Halfway down the motorway, he starts to whinge about needing the toilet. We just tell him to shut up an' it's his fault we are late.

About an hour later, "Right," he says. "I'll show ya", an' he takes off his hard hat, drops his pants then takes a sh#t in it, right there in the back of the van. This is on the motorway only one mile outside of Nottingham. He never even took out the plastic head adjustments. He then put it in a Netto carrier bag, tied the handles together and put that in his workbag.

But that's not the punch line. On the Monday at work, here he is walking into the portakabin with the same hat on! How do we know it was the same hat? Coz it still had his name written in black permanent marker on the back.**"**

The Boro boys are in town.

CHAPTER 2: THE SONGS

Shall we sing a song for you...

The song is the greatest weapon in the arsenal of the away fan. It's obviously important to the home fan as well as in any football match. I like to think it creates an atmosphere unrivalled in sport and is one of the main reasons football stands out as a spectator sport. Other sports have their songs as well but they are not traditionally sung in the same way. Football songs are a chant that can bring a whole stadium together. Get the crowd going and you can get the team going. A single song can make a difference.

The song is what brings supporters together.

Middlesbrough v Manchester United at home. Kevin Keegan had famously been on the telly telling everyone that the title race was not over and that Man U had to "go to Middlesbrough yet an' get a result". He also said "he would love it". Really Kevin?

At this point, a flood warning was issued in the Tees Valley as every Boro supporter pissed themselves laughing. On the fateful day, Boro (led by former Man U captain and club legend Bryan Robson) duly capitulated to the sound of every fan in the ground, home and away, singing "let's all laugh at Keegan... let's all laugh at Keegan na nar nar na" and the now infamous "Hit 'im on the head, hit 'im on the head, hit 'im on the head with a baseball bat Keegan! Keegan!"

But the one we gave them that they sang at Wembley just weeks after was "Cheer up Kevin Keegan" where 35,000 fans all united in one common bond, the singing of the hatred of one little man. The only sour point was the result and the fact that as we walked home you could still hear the away fans singing from inside your own ground… "We're gunna win that football league again… down by the river side, down by the river side". This is something I think will never be sung by our home support in my lifetime. Yet they got to sing it every time they came after that.

The songs we sing at the game are at times like a verbal emotional outpouring of how we feel. When you're away from home getting beat one nil an' it's cold, raining, with the clock on 90+, you start to feel a bit of a mug for going. Now the home support chant the names of their heroes as they run out the match. But then when Boro score an equaliser in the last minute, you burst with joy and the celebration song is sung, either 'Pig Bag' which I personally dislike immensely or 'Chelsea dagger' which I actually hate even more (both were introduced by the club not the fans by the way over the PA system) or even the traditional, unique and far superior "E-I-O", but all are soon eclipsed by the song we all really want to sing… "You're not singing, you're not singing, you're not singing anymore!" Every supporter to a man belts it out with a mixture of relief, aggression and total vindication for actually being there. It's all very playground, childish stuff but it's absolutely brilliant. It is the custard pie in the face of football songs and we all love it.

To me, the best songs are the funny spontaneous songs that are a reaction to the goings-on on or off the pitch.

A good away crowd will sing all the way through a game. It can be a source of constant embarrassment to the home fans. We should know, up until a few years ago the Riverside was an uneasy place to be for a home fan. If we were losing or even nil-nil halfway through the second half, you could have heard a pin drop. This then is when the away supporters would start to take over. Like Chris Evens on the radio, leave a gap between songs and he'll just fill it with the sound of his own voice. It's the same with away fans; they can smell nerves or boo's from the home fans and it's like a call to arms. Next thing you know, you're the fans on the back foot as they cheer their team on, and in the competition of rival chants, playing catch up is a thankless task. Only in the last two or three years have groups like The 12th Man and particularly The Red Faction tried to address this problem. Like it or loath it, I'd still like to hear that drum beat from the south east corner rather than let a bunch of about 600 Portsmouth fans out-sing us at home.

Even Middlesbrough FC have finally got to grips with the idea that away support can make a difference. We must be one of the last clubs to work out it's not such a good idea to have away supporters right behind one of the goals cheering their team on every time they get down that end of the pitch. Clubs like Newcastle have the opposition support tucked away up in the gods where no matter how loud you sing it just gets lost reverberating around the roof. As I understand it, as of next season away fans will be pushed into the south east corner. This will be to all intents and purposes a straight swap with the lads from blocks 53 and around that area. Boro at both ends, just think of that.

That's what watching the Boro away is all about – daft and fun – but that's normally the team on the pitch.

Even in the face of adversity, the ability to take the piss out of yourself can be used to your advantage. I remember the season when the child abuse allegations on multiple families in the area broke on national news. Every away supporter who came would sing songs about us being paedophiles. But then by the time we got to go to their ground, it was us singing songs about getting their kids. Just like the way we have turned around the label of Smog Monsters, we now actually have badges that we wear (with pride, may I add) with a cartoon of a Mr Man called Smoggy.

And we never forget an ex-player, do we? A round of applause for recognition to services given can turn to vicious defamation of character within the space of a bad tackle or even worse, scoring against your old club. I have no time for it. Who cares if he uses the trend of not celebrating when he scores. If he was that bothered, he would have stayed. An' if he was that good, we would have kept him, simple as that.

As the away fan, the song is invaluable. It lets other supporters know who you are ("shall we tell 'em") so you can join or avoid without any problems. You are letting them know 'the Boro boys are in town' so to speak. We can taunt, tease and intimidate while being vastly outnumbered, an' all from behind the relative safety of a thin day-glow line of woefully inadequately trained and undermanned stewards. (The police having priced themselves out of the game years ago).

We don't need no Heath an' Safety,
We don't need no crowd control,
We just want to support the Boro,

HEY! Stewards leave our fans alone!
Because all in all you're just another prick on the dole!
    (RF at their best: a mix of Pink Floyd and Blood
Hound Gang)

Just to push home the point, is it me or have other sports copied the footie chant format? Or have football supporters just starting singing at other sports that they go to watch? Boxing, swimming, cricket, everything now. Even the Olympics have all taken up the football chant. Sure they sang and cheered before but never in the orchestrated way of the football fans. I went to the darts a few years ago at Newcastle Arena and was blown away by the electricity of the place. It was like a boxing match. Each player was introduced like a heavyweight challenger to the baying crowd. It had the feel of what WWF wrestling would be like if it was held in the Munich beer festival. But it was the singing that made it. Indoors the noise was amazing and every player had his song sung by his own section of the fans. It had a 'last day of the season' feel as well, people in fancy dress and a real good nature among the fans. The fans sang all the way through as if every match was the FA Cup final. Well recommended to go to as an out of season distraction from all that transfer and liquidation speculation.

The best example of a chant from the terraces making a difference is the one directed at Jason Lee. If you don't know it, Lee played for Nottingham Forest at the time and used to tie his dreadlock-style hair out of the way high up on his head. But it just happened to come to the attention of comedian and WBA supporter Frank Skinner who mentioned it on the TV show he co-hosted with David Baddiel, Fantasy Football, possibly the best football show ever. The chant, "He's got a pineapple on his head", was taken up by every group of supporters who came to visit. Eventually there was no escape, home or away. He started to react angrily to some sets of fans. Early substitutions and a sudden slump in form quickly followed. Even when he cut his hair, the chant just changed to, "He's lost a pineapple off his head", and he disappeared into obscurity. Supporters are remorseless in their search for that one song that can either inspire or demoralise, just ask Jamie Pollock, but we will keep that for later.

Badges of pride, worn with honour.

Anonerimus

Newcastle v Middlesbrough,
League Cup, 10th October 1990
Score 1-0 (1-2 on agg), Attendance 12,778

"Boro take a 2-0 first leg lead in the Carling Cup to the Toon. Newcastle scored first, mid-way through the first half and then something happens that changes the match and goes down in folk history.

The Toon's battering ram of a striker Mick Quinn gets into a scuffle with Steven Pears when they both go for a loose ball in the box. Quinn looks to walk away then punches Pears full in the face with a sharp right jab. Pears hits the deck like a sack of sh*t, Quinn gets a straight red. This then prompts the travelling Boro fans to start to sing to the tune of the old Mickey Mouse Club theme, "M-i-c... k-e-y... Q-u-i-n-n, Micky Quinn! (Geordie c#n't) Mickey Quinn! (Geordie c#nt)".

Pears recovered to make an amazing acrobatic last minute second half save to take the Boro through.

All that was left was for us to somehow get to the train station without getting killed. **"**

Anonerimus

Chester v Middlesbrough,
Third Division, 2nd May 1987
Score 1-2, Attendance 3,788

"It was not a bad drive down and the support was bigger than we all expected. Loads of cars and buses with the tell-tale Boro scarves out the window or the old TFM Boro sticker. It's a funny ground, a bit like a prefabricated industrial building for light industry. Anyway, the support was so good by the time kick off came around, we had filled the whole of one end. This away end was covered but only in the middle and even then only about three quarters down, but the corners were completely exposed and it was not a warm day by any stretch.

Half way through the first half, it starts. The sky darkened and the rain started to fall, slow random rain drops well spaced out but the size of golf balls. Within about five minutes, it's bouncing off the heads of the people stood in front of us who are just beyond the edge of the sheds covering. Everyone is now squeezing as far as they can to get in under the pitiful corrugated iron roofing. But it's no good, there are way too many crammed into the end to get everyone under. By the second half, those stood in the exposed corners are totally soaked through and with the rain still hammering down they are left with only one thing to do. They start to do the conga. Then piss about a bit doing little songs like, "we're singing in the rain, just singing in the rain". They get a great round of applause for that. Then all the fans outside of the covering turn in on our own fans with their backs to the game and are singing and pointing in great waves to our own support singing. "We're all wet, we're all wet, you're not, you're not!" This went on for a good 20 minutes. It was just daft and defiant and most of all fun an' it makes me smile now thinking about it.**"**

Anonerimus

Arsenal v Middlesbrough,
Premier League, 14th January 2006
Score 7-0, Attendance 38,186

(I have had a number of fans tell me this one in different guises but this was the best.)

"Go down to Arsenal an' it's all "geezer, geezer, geezer" an' "knock it on the 'ed", an' all that. Highbury was full to the brim as usual. We met up with some of Supporters South at the Swiss Cottage for a few beers before, so spirits were high. We have had some great matches with them through the years and are looking forward to it. Who could forget the 5-3 game in 2004 when we were 3-1 up. This was not going to be one of them games. The saying 'run ragged' doesn't cover the way they played. Too soon it became the Henry and Fabregas Show, a lesson dealt out to us northern scum. But that's not what sticks in my mind.

The Boro fans were amazing that day. When the score got to 3-0 and it was obvious that it was going to be a long afternoon, remembering the game in 2004 we started to sing, "We're gunna win 3-4, we're gunna win 3-4'. But then every time they scored again we just changed the song, so that in the end we found ourselves singing "7-8, we're gunner win 7-8" but bored with this now, the last chant and the one my mate who is an Arsenal fan always talks about, is "8-nil, we're gunner lose 8-nil, we're gunner loose 8-nil", much to the amusement of the Ars. But the thing is, I can't remember anyone leaving early, probably coz it cost so much for a ticket an' we're all tight twats. **"**

Anonerimus

Hull v Middlesbrough,
Championship, 9th April 2012
Score 2-1, Attendance 19,163

"If you've never been t'Hull then you've not lived. What a waste ground. Some of it is even sh*tter than here. Apart from the number of pubs on Bev Road, it's got f*ck all. But we did get a good little player from them; that Nicky Barmy, he was smart like. Him, Juninho and Hignett they called 'em the 'midget gems'.

We went down when he was manager there an' a think some sections of the crowd had had enough of him. See, after he left us (the rumour was that he was having problems at home if ya know what I'm talking about), every time he came back with another club we had a special song for him. Obviously this time it's better coz he's the manager. Anyway, we always take a good number down to Hull and as soon as the game got going we started singing, "Stand up if ya shagged Barmby's wife, stand up if ya shagged Barmby's wife." Everyone is already standing with their arms stretched out, but then the Hull supporters start standing up and singing it too, f*cking mental or what? Should have known his time was up right there and then, mate. I'm sure half their supporters think we play with a wrong-shaped ball anyway. **"**

Tee - Tee - Teessiders!

Anonerimus

Norwich v Middlesbrough,
Premier League, 31st October 1992
Score 1-1, Attendance 14,499

" I went down to Norwich for the game. The only reason I went was because I had mates who are at uni down there. Norwich is a nice place and a good night out as well. But it's a bit out of the way and the locals look a bit funny. It must be the low horizons and all that interbreeding.

Like I said, it's a bit out of the way and I don't think we took up the full ticket allocation. Still we had plenty to make some good noise. But when they start singing, "Come in a taxi, ya should have come in a taxi", I thought now that's rich, beause when we looked around the place, it was hardly full to the brim. So our fans applaud back ironically. Then they sing it again. Well, that was once too many for the Boro fans. Just as they finish "Come in a taxi" for the last time, someone starts singing and we all join in as loud as we can. "Come in ya sister, ya shouldn't come in ya sister."

Makes you proud to be from Loftus. **"**

All the Geordies went to Rome just to see the Pope.

CHAPTER 3: THE TRANSPORT

Come in a taxi...

Now then, you nicked off work and waited in the rain outside Ayresome Park for over two hours to get your tickets at the start of the week. It's then taken almost military precision and a huge leap of faith (in the time before mobiles) that everyone who said they were going two weeks ago are actually still going to turn up and more importantly pay you for them. You are stood at the train station, outside a pub, working men's club or in Eston swimming baths car park. You have a warm coat with you even in the summer "coz ya never know". You have a canvas rucksack by your side, holding a tartan flask and a Tuppaware box with sandwiches in it or a plastic Co-op bag with a four pack of McEwan's Red Death and a quarter of wine gums. The one thing you have in common as you wait is the anticipation of whether you can actually get there and back? Will British Rail screw you over at Doncaster and miss the connection? Will it be a Bee Line luxury coach or a Walter's school bus that smells of sick at the back? In my case it was always, "Please let Steve have borrowed his dad's Cortina" as everyone but Steve knows, you can't actually get four people in a Capri.

Think about it: if you owned a coach company or even a mini

bus, would you hire out to a bunch of football supporters? I know a van hire company who are reluctant to even let you have a Transit over the weekend if you so much as have an Up The Boro sticker in your car window. Don't get me wrong, some companies know the score and charge accordingly and I'm sure that the Official Supporters Club have had a good relationship with many coach firms over the years. It's just that some of the ones I've had the misfortune to use have been, well, dangerous. There are the ones that you sleep all the way to the ground, spark out like a baby, only to find that that funny diesel smell the driver told you not to worry about was actually the exhaust fumes coming in under the back seat.

One of the worst outcomes of the football violence in the 70s and 80s was the introduction of the 'Dry Train' and the ban on alcohol in away coaches. This led to hundreds of new and innovative ways of hiding, consuming and generally trying to circumnavigate any checks for alcohol from the police. Coach drivers became almost like racketeers, taking back handers in the form of a 'whip round' with the selling point of "Oh if I get caught I will lose me licence". Actually all that happened when you were stopped was that the police just took great pleasure in confiscating all your booze then escorting the coach back to Middlesbrough, or the other favoured trick was to stop you and then to radio a person's check through for every single supporter on the coach, making you so late you would miss the kick off anyway. So special routes had to be designed to either avoid the police checks or find a number of fan-friendly pubs on the way. The problem with this was it took longer, cost more and left you open to rival supporter aggro in country pubs in the middle of nowhere which ironically is the one time you actually want the police to turn up. Fans will try anything from mixing JD with a litre bottle of coke and putting it in their kid's bag, to gaffer-taping balloons full of shots to their body like some kind of crap vodka drugs mule. Some coach drivers were supporters too and would let you put your beer in the luggage hold under the bus. We had a lad who would then put a piece of laminated board up to section it off so even if the police took a look, it would look like it was empty. We never knew what it was used for when the Boro were at home and didn't want to ask to tell the truth, but we started a rumour that he did a lot of 'weekend trips to Amsterdam' nod nod wink wink.

For me, the best way to travel away is by train. I know some people who can't stand it, but nothing compares to the atmosphere. You can have a nice little table for your own clique of friends, a few beers, a pie from the buffet, maybe a wander along the carriage, see some faces and have a chat. But best of all, go to the toilet in relative safety. Unlike the car or coach, you don't have to sit doubled up in pain thinking about Stuart Boam just to take your mind off the fact that you need a wee. I've been on a bus where it's just a mad sprint from one service station to another and even a lay-by or two all the way to the ground. Also by train you don't get that edgy moment when other supporters crisscrossing the country to their own away matches suddenly all converge on Tamworth services. You do get other supporters on the trains but to be fair the British Transport police (god bless 'em) keep the carriages separate most of the time. But the best thing of all is that the long cylinder shape of the train carriages makes for some of the best pre-match singing ever. Your ears can still be ringing well after it's all calmed down. I also love the way people are more friendly. If they have a tray of Stella in front of them, they will offer you one. If you're on your own, they will engage you in conversation and as we all know, nothing breaks down barriers quicker than talking about football. Next thing you know you've had three cans, you both know 'Yeti' from Brompton and you're pulling into your destination. Here the police are waiting to give you a ceremonial guard of honour to that big shed in the middle of nowhere.

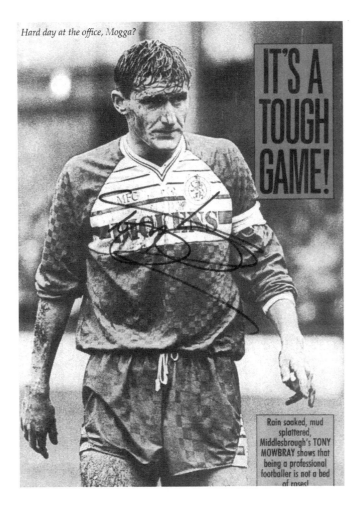

Hard day at the office, Mogga?

IT'S A TOUGH GAME!

Rain soaked, mud splattered, Middlesbrough's TONY MOWBRAY shows that being a professional footballer is not a bed of roses!

Anonerimus

Newcastle v Middlesbrough,
Premier League, 1st May 1999
Score 1-1, Attendance 36,552

"I have a message for all away supporters. Do not go by car if you are going to leave the stickers from the garage you bought it from in the back window.

We went to the Newcastle game and parked up at the Tesco at Kinky Park, near the Falcons' ground. Then we got the Metro into the Toon. When we got back after the game, someone had written anti-smoggie slogans all over the car, in… wait for it… banana! The skins had then been placed like hood ornaments on the bonnet. The smell on the drive home was nice but it was a f*cking bast*rd to get off the next morning.**"**

Travelling in style.

Smoggies on tour.

Anonerimus

QPR v Middlesbrough,
Premier League, 2nd December 1995
Score 0-0, Attendance 17,546

" At the Tamworth service station on our way back from a long trip down to QPR, from one of the cubicals in the bloke's bogs comes this almighty sloppy fart noise.

We and the people stood just pissin' go, "Ughhhhh" in disgust.

Then there's another great fart and a sloppy squirting noise louder than before and in a broad Boro accent comes, "F*ckin' hell Jesus Christ."

We all laugh. Then again the same long fart and splattering sounds, he then shouts, "Please someone call an ambulance. I'm sh*ttin' meself to death here. Oh god, the smell… my eyes, my eyes are burning… Son? Son, if ya still there, can ya call ahead to ya mam an' get her to put some toilet paper in the freeza for us."

I'll never forget the chemical-like acid stench of that toilet ever. **"**

Anonerimus

Chelsea v Middlesbrough,
FA Cup Final, 17th May 1997
Score 2-0, Attendance 79,160

"My boss told us about his mate who was desperate to go to the FA Cup final. He tried all over to get a ticket and eventually paid a small fortune from some rip off merchant. So he books himself on the same coach leaving Boro early on the day of the game with his mates. Now this lad is sh*t at getting up in the morning and some of the lads he's going with are his work mates and he's always late for work. He's one of these people who when you ask him where he is, he's like, "I'm on my way, just getting in the taxi now" and then turns up two hours later. They are all telling him that it's setting off really early to make it in good time for a drink. They try time and again to persuade him to go by train. But no, he wants to go with them and he's paid over the odds for his ticket so he's going down with his mates. So he hatches a plan. He knows he's rubbish at getting up so as the coach is setting off at 5am in the morning, he'll just stay up all night at his mam's and sleep on the coach on the way down.

Brilliant, I hear you say, what a simple foolproof plan. What could possibly go wrong? So he gets a good night's sleep the night before, takes the day before off work and then gets himself a load of snacks, Lucozade drinks and a bunch of DVDs to keep him awake. Well, you guessed it, he's a no show at the pickup point next morning and everyone's like "told ya so" and they can't ring him coz they haven't got his mam's number. Some of the lads even put bets on him not turning up. They are just coming along in between Northallerton and Thirsk when they hear this beeping of a car horn. They look out of the window and here he is in his dad's car, blearing the horn and flashing his lights driving along the side of the coach.

Eventually they persuade the driver to pull over as he's weaving about in front of the bus now trying to get it to stop. They pull up in a lay-by in the middle of nowhere and he gets out of the car.

"Are you on your own?" they ask.

"Yea, me dad's not up yet so a just borrowed his car."

"What? Are ya just gunna leave it here?"

"Yea, be all reet I'll pick it up on the way back tonight."

So he tells them that he fell asleep watching Forest Gump. He thought a good long movie over three hours long would keep him up… errr no. He calms down and is just sat having a can when he says, "Thank f*ck it was you lot. I'm not sure I could do that again." They look at each other. "Again?" "Oh yea, I stopped a coach just before the Stokesley turn off… it was full of f*cking pensioners from Stockton going to York for the day." Our kid says, "Ya joking, arn ya?" "I know," he says, "there'll be nowt open when they get there, stupid or what?" He has loads of other stories about this lad but none football-related unfortunately. 🤚

Anonerimus

Middlesbrough v WBA,
Championship, 29th November 1997
Score 1-0, Attendance 30,164

Man U v Blackburn,
Premier League, 30th November 1997
Score 4-0, Attendance 55,175

"I'm on the train heading back to Boro to go home for me dad's funeral (he had a heart attack after the WBA game). Needless to say I'm not 100%. The train stops at Northallerton and a lad in a Man U shirt jumps on an' asks dead quick, "Is this the Edinburgh train?"

"Yea mate," I reply and he shouts out the door and his mate also in a Man U shirt gets on, parking themselves on the opposite table to me. They both have that bright-eyed look that young Man U supporters who are not from Manchester have, even down to the clean crisp freshly ironed (by the mam) new season Man U shirt.

I compliment them, like chalk and cheese with my red with white writing M'BRO woolly hat on (this is just an UMBRO hat with the 'U' cut out an' then stitched back up). They are a little too happy for my own state of mind. Like two excited puppies on their first walk down the road.

The lad asks another question, "Going to the match, mate?"

Now you know an' I know, he has no interest in whether I'm going to the match or not. He just wants to tell me they 'are' going to the match.

"No. You?" I ask through gritted teeth.

"Yea it's our first game."

Now I'm interested. Dressed like they are, I wonder how long they will last when they get off the train, so a little concerned I ask, "Where you off to then, St James's or Stadium of Sh#te?"

"Oh no, Blackburn at home," he says.

I nearly pissed meself.

"This is the train to Edinburgh not from Edinburgh… you were on the north platform side, not the south side."

They look at me blankly.

"You're on the wrong train, lads."

As I changed trains at Darlo, I thought to myself how the old man would have loved that. He could never understand why people didn't support their local team.

"Serves 'em right an' all, the daft buggers," he would have said. **"**

All roads lead to Wembley!

Anonerimus

Bolton v Middlesbrough,
League Cup Final, 29th February 2004
Score 1-2, Attendance 72,634

"The bus we got to go to Cardiff was hired from a company through work. The driver arrived late and wouldn't wait any longer for anyone who was not there by the time we had loaded up. He insisted that all booze was locked in the luggage boot. Because "I'm not losing my license for anyone". He wouldn't put the radio on and only scheduled stops at service stations. It was as if everything he did was just to spoil the whole event. After what was an age we arrive in our over night at Bristol gagging for a beer. It took more than one or two blokes to get this driver to open up the boot and let us get to our beer, he was being a right dick.

Next day not so bad but still he insisted in the beer being locked away. As it happened he was right, the police were waiting for us to escort us into Cardiff and we had to alight with the police still escorting us by foot into the centre. Obviously the game was great but we couldn't stay and drink for too long as the driver had made it clear he was setting off on time regardless of stragglers. In fact, he actually left two lads behind. So as we were getting on, we voiced our disapproval and he said it was a good job there wasn't extra time or we would all be left behind.

Then when we got back, he would not drop off on the way in like Yarm or Ingleby Barwick. He would only drop off at the same one pick up point. Obviously there was no collection and heated words were exchanged before he drove off. But he even had the last laugh. He took all the beer that was in the boot from that morning, thieving bastard. A few days later when we went to complain, we found out that the coach company was a Sunderland firm. And the driver was a Mackem supporter. He must have tried his best to spoil our day, but feck him, we won hahahah.**"**

CHAPTER 4:
THE BEER

Beer, beer, we want more beer...

Once upon a not so long ago, drinking and going to the match were inseparable; pint before and a pint after. A pub was always a good place for people to meet before games especially for the away supporter. A recognised public place in a strange town to get out of the cold and look less conspicuous. The word would always go out of the names of the pubs that were safe to go in and the ones that were say a Millwall pub. Once a good number of away fans have found their way to the designated destination of congregation, there is an unspoken tipping point whereupon the noise level changes, the accents get thicker and spontaneous bouts of chanting take place. This will get louder and louder as the bar staff get edgier and then Dave the landlord suddenly appears making small talk and asking if everything is okay. I always feel sorry for the bar staff. There can only be so many times you can be told "Ow much? It's only £1.80 in the Beechwood & Easterside club" before you snap and start rubbing the rim of the 'clean' glasses out the back round the rim of your bellend. A quick note to all landlords across the country DO NOT put young lasses on bar duty on a match day. (I feel no need to explain this last statement).

Just getting served away from home can be turned into a challenge of the kind of magnitude like when Captain Cook stopped off to ask some islanders for a barrel of water and a bit of fresh fruit. I think we have all heard the story of the bloke who asked for half a coke in a London pub and was brought half a cork.

Armed with this knowledge, I was in a pub in Swindon with my father-in-law and as he went to get the round in, I told him (as he was driving) that if he wanted a coke he should ask for a 'Coca-Cola' not just a coke. After an age, he came back with the drinks. I asked him if it was busy at the bar? "No," he said. It just took him 20 minutes to convince the barman he really did want a half a lime and lemon and then another 10 minutes to convince him it was an actual drink an' not some genetically modified 'limon'. Mind, we don't help ourselves, do we? Deliberately asking for a Bottle of Dog will just antagonise an already on edge landlord.

There is a story, that became a rumour, that has now moved through urban myth into football folklore and that is that at the Coca-Cola Cup final at Wembley, Boro became the first and only fans to drink their half of the ground dry... before kickoff. Not only that but we did it again in the FA Cup only weeks later (I know! They should have learned their lesson right an' got more booze).

I was there along with many thousands of Boro fans who had the same experience. They did actually run out of bottled beers, but they did have some more by half time. I have always put this down to the fact that it was our first major cup final and everyone just went straight to the ground, meaning we drank for longer before kick off. But then when the FA Cup came round, I remember thinking, what again? Who do they get in to run the bar? The committee of the Dorman's Club? They could have made a fortune. I also totally accept that this was what it was like for every club. But no, Chelsea fans had no such problems. Should we be proud of this fact? Is it a fact at all? We can't prove it or disprove it. But if a fan from another club asks if it's true, I just shrug and say, "Apparently so, you soft southern shandy drinking sh*te", an' leave it at that.

It's just like the Geordies can't prove we threw Mars Bars at Gazza when he came to take a corner at Ayresome Park. Their urban myth is that he picked one up and took a bite. Well, if he had, he would have broken his teeth as they were all empty packets full of stones. I like our version better.

The year of that double Wembley appearance spurned a Song of Songs which was unique as it used not the word 'Mum' but 'Mam' as in 'Me Mam' and it's a song I would give our lasses back teeth to sing again.

"Tell ya mam ya mam, t' put the champagne on ice, we're goin' t' Wembley twice, tell ya mam, tell ya mam". (Poetry in its purest form).

Typically we managed to incorporate the joy of going to Wembley with every Boro supporter's other two great loves, drinking and taking the piss out of ourselves (like we would waste good money on French fizzy sugar water). Sorry, and a third thing, the love of our mams obviously. Some of the best songs are alcohol-related with lines like, "We all drink whisky and Newcastle Brown… the Boro boys are in town" and the world famous, tub thumping, foot stamping, "Beer, beer, we want more beer, all the lads a singin' 'Get the f*cking beer in'. Beer, beer, we want more beer". It's a great chant and even better in a pub with loads of lads banging their empty glasses in time on the tables.

The beer around the country is so different, isn't it? I'm lucky to have lived in different parts of the country and sampled many, many local brews over prolonged periods. The thing that strikes me is that other people like their beer completely opposite to us and this is more evident the further south you get. Just to clarify, a pint of beer should be dark, full bodied with a bitter aftertaste, a little lively in the glass so as to give a thick creamy head and lastly it should be slightly below room temperature to make it refreshing. But the further south you get, the lighter, sweeter, flatter and warmer it gets. If you are in Wiltshire, it also has a soapy taste to it. Apparently they have hard water; must be the only thing that is. When in London drinking beer, remember the water they make it with has been through lots and lots of other people first before it makes its way to you, if you know what I mean.

Boro have a long association with beer and a lot to be thankful for. Remember the McEwan's 80 Bob invisible clock with its 'It's McEwan's time' or the classic Cameron-sponsored shirt as well as our own crowning glory, the Carling Cup.

Beer has fuelled, sponsored and ultimately been the downfall of many a football event with the invention of the English lager lout, our greatest football export. The ultimate away supporter stereotype, the English football hooligan and his weapon of choice; a thrown empty beer bottle or a white plastic garden chair. The classic BBC news line would always start with "Trouble erupted after English fans who had been drinking all day in bars around the plaza…" Dark, dark days for all. But for every one negative incident, you could point out thousands of fans from all around the country and the world chatting, singing and most of all, laughing over a beer in some far off bar.

Anonerimus

Chelsea v Middlesbrough,
League Cup Final, 29th March 1998
Score 2-0, Attendance 77,698

" On the 'Dry Train' on the way down to the final, the police are checking people's bags for booze with the warning: "Anyone found with alcohol on them or drunk on the train will be detained at London King's Cross and will miss the match". We have an empty seat on our table as we pull out. After about ten minutes this big man-mountain of a skinhead comes wondering down the train banging off the side of seats as he comes. He's had a right skin full and looks like he's still out from the night before. He stops and plonks himself into the spare seat. Plonks a carrier bag on the table and without a word, takes out one Pyrex glass bowl and one pack of Kellogg's variety cereals. These are all different types of cereals in little boxes. And a 1 litre bottle of chocolate milk. He then empties all the cereals into the bowl followed by the litre of chocolate milk. He puts all the empty boxes in the bag with the empty plastic bottle and put it on the over head. He then takes a massive dessert spoon out of the inside pocket of his Harrington jacket and tucks right in. It's now very apparent that the chocolate milk is actually Baileys Irish Cream. The man is a total genius. After a while, I have to ask him, "What if the conductor comes along?" They'll throw you off."

An' he goes, "Nor, I haven't even got a f*cking ticket."

I try again, "An' a ya not bothered about the police holding ya at King's Cross then if they catch ya? You'll miss the match."

"I haven't even got a ticket for the f*cking game, mate. A'm only going for the crack like."

Like I said, the man was a total genius.**"**

Anonerimus

Dumbarton v Middlesbrough,
Pre-season, 23rd July 2009
Score 0-5, Attendance not available

"Pre-season trip to Dumbarton, we have no idea why but it just seemed like a good idea at the time. We took this long spotty streak with us, the friend of one of the lad's son's. He was having trouble keeping up with the rounds and by the time we were about to go to the game he was a full pint behind.

As we all finished off, he was just standing there with this full pint still in his hand, weaving slightly, totally out of it. "Leave it if you want, mate, no bother," I remember someone saying. I can't remember saying it as I was halfway gone myself to be honest but apparently I said something like, "Go on, get it down ya, ya girl," so he took a deep breath and downed it in one, slamming his glass on the table defiantly.

We all cheered and turned to leave when he snatches up the glass again and vomits right back into it filling it right to the brim then he put it down, waits a moment, picks up another empty pint and vomits into that, filling it almost right to the top. After the initial cries of disgust, the place goes silent and he straightens up and says dead quietly, "Two for one… an' it's not even happy hour."

I put my arm round him and led him outside; this was obviously a legend in the making we had here.**"**

Boro 'LDC' Line Dancing Crew meet Boro away

Anonerimus

Burnley v Middlesbrough,
League Division One, 18th December 1994
Score 0-3, Attendance 12,049

"One time at the Burnley Working Men's Club as a line of about 100 Boro supporters enter one after another after another, the committee man on the door was left open-mouthed. As each one passed, they said pointing to the one following. "He's signing me in", or "Soz mate forgot me card", or "Is subs this week or next week", and we just kept on coming in until it was rammed. But they had the last laugh as they must have taken a fortune in beer and crisps sales.

At one point they had to drop the shutters on the bar to stop us from serving ourselves because the bar was so deep with Boro fans. One lad even bought a full one of them hanging card trays of pork scratchings and then left just three hanging on it to cover the modesty of the half naked lady pictured underneath. A little touch of Boro class. **"**

Anonerimus

Man U v Middlesbrough,
Premier League, 29th January 2005
Score 2-0, Attendance 67,251

"There's this lad you probably know. He has about ten different names but you would know him if you seen him out drinking. The company he worked for once sponsored the match ball at the Riverside and when they went to get their photos took, all suited and booted for a corporate day, he was mistaken for Macaroni. Ended up signing autographs, shaking hands with fans. That's totally true by the way and that would just be a normal day for this lad.

But that's not the story I want to tell you. He's on another corporate day out at Old Trafford and on his way driving home, when he suddenly wakes up sat on the floor with a lorry driver talking to him. He looks up and his beamer is upside down a few yards away in the middle of a field somewhere off the A19. When the police arrive and start talking to him, he tells them how much he's had to drink that day, "I had a bottle of Peroni with the sponsor about 11.30, then two glasses of wine with my meal, another bottle of non-descript lager at half time. Then after the game one more before heading off."

Not too bad in a seven hour period with a meal as well. Oh, then he tells them he had a few flaming Sambucas on his way home.

"I blame that last flaming Sambuca," he says.

The policeman asks him if he is admitting to being over the limit. "No way," he says, "it takes more than a Sambuca to get me drunk. It's just that they're a bast*rd to light on the dash at 80mph."

If you know him and you're reading this, you know this is a very frightening and a very true story.**"**

Anonerimus

Millwall v Middlesbrough, League Division One,
26th February 1995 • Score 0-0, Attendance 7,247

"Every Boro fan knows that a trip down to London will at some time start with the early morning wander around Darlington Train Station and the Edinburgh to London King's Cross train.

We were doing just this on our way down to Millwall when we could hear singing coming from the northbound platform. We had about twenty minutes so we took a look. There was a group of lads (not in colours) just messing around drinking cans with one lad asleep on a metal bench. We got chatting and they told us they had come up from 'darn sarf' on a stag and they were planning to stay in Whitley Bay, drink there during the day then go into Newcastle's Big Market on the night and wanted to know all about it.

But they had come a cropper of the guard who had chucked them off because the stag had been sick and passed out. We could see the station guards were giving them the eye from a safe distance. Said stag was the gent laid on the bench in an Arsenal shirt. They told us he was indeed a Gooner and was gutted he was missing the match. We wished them luck then wandered back to our platform when they announced the King's Cross train was about to arrive. Now back then you could get from one platform to another via the central shared toilets. As we made ourselves comfortable in our seats, it was from these toilets that four of the stag party came walking very fast. One was carrying a bag, the other two were carrying the stag by his arms over their shoulders dragging his feet behind. They just walked straight onto the train, dumped him in a chair on the opposite table, plonked his bag on his lap then jumped off as the train door beeped and closed. As we pulled away, they stood waving to us.

We didn't stop laughing until after York when our tickets were checked. The conductor took it in his stride when we told him and he told us to let him know via the buffet car when our 'friend' woke up. I think he woke up about Peterborough, I'm not sure, but I do know he was grateful for a tea and a sandwich when he did. We said good bye to him at King's Cross as he left us to try and get on another train up north.**"**

CHAPTER FIVE: THE FOOD

Who ate all the pies? You fat...

Ah, the smell of cheap boiled hot dogs and fried burgers with onions. I like them from a van with that little element of danger. I remember a bloke who used to have a sort of hand cart that sold hot dogs and hamburgers (what ever happened to hamburgers?) outside Ayresome Park and then again on a night outside the Mad House until about three in the morning. We called him the 'sunny salmonella man' (we even had a story about him).

Most places you visit have their own equivalent little man in a van and it's a welcome sight and smell after travelling or drinking all morning. A welcome hot meal after the crisps and Ginsters pasties of the motorway services. I once went a full 24 hours on just Ginsters, Walkers crisps and Timmy Taylors Landlord beer. God, did I pay for it the next day and so did my workmates. What you need when away from home is something to soak up all that beer. Something not just from a van after a few lagers. A warm healthy meal inside you like the classic Wetherspoon's burger and a pint, the nutritional cornerstone of any breakfast.

Once you're inside the ground, you are at the mercy of the club caterers. Not so bad if you're Norwich and the chairperson is Delia Smith. The only culinary delight our lot ever came up with was the mythical Juninho Burger, that's a beef burger with salsa sauce, thanks for that, lads. I'm still not convinced it ever existed. Sunderland reckon they were the first to do the chicken balti pie inside the ground but I think they will find that Scottish clubs had a good two years on them. The pie is still the benchmark to which the footballing foodies set their standard. So much so that the coveted Best Pie competition is hotly disputed and supported by the official supporters clubs as well as the FA. Who could forget the pie scandal of the 2011-2012 season when Arsenal won the coveted Football Pie of the Year, collecting over 8,500 votes. On the night of the ceremony, many were amazed to see the club's official Emirates caterers going up to collect the award. In fact, many of the votes accrued had been for Piebury Corner, a husband an' wife team who sell from an independent stall outside the ground. Last year's winners were Morecambe Football club, where the Head Chef Graham Aimson said he just wanted to maintain the tradition of good British food. Never mind a pie award, give that man an OBE or even a Knighthood.

As a kid I remember the first time our dad took me to the match, it was cold and we got Bovril or Oxo, I'm not sure which. But I do remember the packet of plain crisps he bought me. The bag was massive in my hands and he told me they were special crisps you could only get at the match. The Bovril was too hot for me an' I couldn't drink it. So he told me it was okay and to dip my crisps into it with a wink like he was letting me in on some secret. I remember that salty beefy taste even now and for me that's the taste of football.

Years later I found out he was right, the crisps were called

Chip Monk and they actually made a specially large bag only sold in football grounds.

When I lived in Newcastle, I refused to go to the Toon games so I would go on the Metro to see Whitley Bay. Funny little club but well ran with a good bar. They did food in the club house, nothing fancy but stuff like pie and chips, hot pot, that sort of thing. They had a chip van as well, parked just inside the gate, which every now and then would sell something called whiting which are tiny little fish battered with the heads still on and served like a bag of chips with a bit of salt an' vinegar. They were sick but the locals loved them, you could see them scoffing them down an' he'd be sold out in no time. Like I said, funny little club. Still I had three great days out at Wembley on the bounce with them in the FA Vase, with a win each time. Proper old school supporters, the town was emptied every time.

Mostly now food at the football is all the same, no matter where you go. It's that mass catering standard, slightly over-priced and they always run out of pies before half time at the away end. I want to see new things when I go away. When I go to Grimsby, I want fish an' chip vans. When I go to Birmingham, I want a stall selling me curry and rice with a nan. It may be stereotypical and regionalist but at the very least when you come to Boro, we give you a Parmo.

Anonerimus

*York v Middlesbrough,
Third Division, 1st January 1987
Score 3-1, Attendance 8,611*

"We only went to York so we could go into town for a drink afterwards. We get dressed smart like a race day and get the train down. It was packed with Boro supporters, must have taken thousands down with us. Before we get on the train we load up with bottles of Brown and some Upex pies. Now, I have a very nice gray jacket on with little black and silver flecks in it that I used to roll the sleeves up, cool as, think John Taylor out of Duran Duran.

I put my pies wrapped in brown bags in each of my jacket pockets. Like I said, the train down was a laugh and we sat eating our pies and drinking our bottles. The game was sh*t but it was a lot of good players and lads from the youth team about to come good. York was a great night out and we just made the last train home. We slept most of the way an' as we pulled into Middlesbrough Station, I picked up my jacket to put it on. One side felt a bit heavy as I swung it to put my arm in the sleeve. When I smoothed out the jacket, I looked down an' there on the right hand side where the nice silver trimmed pocket used to be was a big brown greasy stain the size of a dinner plate. I'd forgot I'd left my last pie in my jacket pocket and it must have been crushed when I was asleep, I thought, but no, my mate told me, it had been like that after the match and it had been getting slowly bigger as the gravy had seeped out as we went round York. What a git! He could have told me. I was walking round York looking like a cock. That jacket was £55 and I was only on £45 a week apprentice wage as well. Totally gutted. My mate said he asked me if I still wanted the pie coz he'd have it if not? But I can't remember that like, I'd have smacked him.**"**

Anonerimus

Rochdale v Middlesbrough,
Freight Rover Trophy, 10th February 1987
Score 0-0 (3-4 on pen), Attendance 2,615

"They had like a stall inside the ground an' they didn't do burgers or chips, they did meat and potato pies, mushy peas and pickled red cabbage that you helped yourself to from a plastic bucket at the end of counter. It was spectacular and even better was the chalked sign that just said, "No, we don't do gravy".**"**

Tranmere v Middlesbrough,
League Division Two, 10th April 1992
Score 1-2, Attendance 8,842

"If you ever went to Tranmere in the early 90s, then you would have seen one of the best burger stalls ever. When we went, the queue was about 20 deep and no one was in a hurry at the front. We could hear lots of laughing and loads of raised cheery voices but could not see what was going on. It took an age to get served but when we did, it was worth it. There behind the counter were three of the best looking lasses you would ever see. Jet black curly hair piled high on their heads, lots of Arabian glow make-up, thick bright red lipstick with tight red uniforms, and best of all was the fact that they were sisters and you could tell it a mile off. The fact that they had made the effort to look so good to sell burgers to testosterone-fuelled males probably did their egos the world of good. But to us after travelling all the way from Middlesbrough, it was a little bit of glamour in one of the crappest grounds in the north west.**"**

Anonerimus

"This one is for all the poor away fans that came to visit us in the 80s and 90s. Do you remember the hot dog cart that was always outside the Madhouse on a Friday night? He did hot dogs and boiled hamburgers with onions (can you still get boiled hamburgers by the way?). Every Saturday you would wake up with the sh*ts thinking it was too much cheap beer. But on a Saturday afternoon there he would be outside the away end at Ayresome Park selling the leftovers from the night before to the unsuspecting away fans. I would always think, if the Boro didn't get ya the Sunny salmonella man would, but not until they were about half way home on the coach. Imagine that, the long trip back down to Portsmouth on a coach with no toilet has just got a whole lot longer. **"**

Sheff Wed v Middlesbrough,
Championship, 4th May 2013
Score 2-0, Attendance 31,375

"I bought a pie at Sheff Wed an' it was disgusting so a took it back to the boiler behind the counter and told her our lass's gash tasted better.

"Gash?" she said.

"Yea, gash," a said back, big smile on my face.

"What's gash? Is it a northern delicacy, is it?"

"Oh yea," I said. "Like hairy fish pie."

She stood looking at me with a blank face, so a just walked back to the lads in total disbelief. **"**

£2 for chips but you do get a carton to throw away for free.

Anonerimus

Chelsea v Middlesbrough,
FA Cup Final, 17th May 1997
Score 2-0, Attendance 79,160

" After the FA Cup final, we had arranged to meet up with some Boro lads who had moved down to London years ago for the work. They'd not gone to the match and we hadn't seen them for years, so we were wondering if we would recognise them or if they had lost their accents an' all that sort of thing.

As we entered the Indian restaurant we arranged to meet in, I started to look around to see if I could see them. At first we started to think they were a no show an' then from one of the tables in the corner we heard, "Ow love have ya got anymore of them massive crisps, like."

Ya can take the lad out of the Boro but... **"**

CHAPTER SIX: THE AWAY GROUND

Nice ground, sh*t fans...

Ayresome Park, even through the rose-tinted glasses of our most hardened supporters, was never a beautiful ground. It was though a classic in its own right. It was a tight little ground with a capacity of 26,667 but at some matches after playing our anthem, the Power Game theme, Bernard (middle name 'a true') Gent would announce the size of the crowd and you'd think, what? Where did the other 3,000 to 5,000 disappear to off the attendance? You could actually see more than that right in front of you. Then the rumour would go round that the club would be holding back cash from the taxman... only a rumour obviously.

Now of course at the Riverside it's the other way round, they read it out with a basic number of season tickets holders as a starting point and you look around at all the empty seats thinking surely, 3,000 supporters can't all be at the bar.

But it was not until you travelled away from that little red and white jewel glowing in the night amongst the dirty dark brown street houses that you started to appreciate what we had, with four covered sides, three sides seated, and no gaping holes in the corners, 360 degrees of gleaming cheering faces. Compare that to some of the grounds we visited well into the 80s like Barnsley, Wigan, Burnley. Then the supposed bigger clubs like Sunderland and Newcastle with their open terraces and uncovered ends. A lot of these clubs stayed like this and didn't change until the late 90s.

Some grounds you could hear a pin drop. Like famously in Old Trafford you could see their mouths move and their arms wave in unison but no sound. I always thought it was because we were making so much noise that you couldn't hear the opposition. But no, every away supporter from different clubs has said the same. If I remember rightly though Middlesbrough v Chesterfield in the cup semi final at Old Trafford the noise was deafening, not just from us but from those amazing and sadly robbed Chesterfield fans. Now there's a thing, how many other sets of away fans would wander the pubs and streets around the ground saying "sorry" to the opposite fans. Only Boro away fans could salvage some pride out of an embarrassing day for all, including the ref.

But some grounds take your breath away. Wembley (old and new) personally didn't do it for me, though I've talked to lots of supporters who say it was the best ground they had ever visited. With all its faults, it's still a dream-come-true location for lots of fans. For me it was the Millennium Stadium in Cardiff. With its steep sides and the whole idea of the closed roof, it just has the best atmosphere; you're quick in, quick out and straight into the city centre. Whoever planned, designed and built that stadium should be on free Yates' beer vouchers for life.

Some just look great. I've been a fan of the arched stands of the Reebok stadium, Bolton, for years. I remember when it was built, thinking 'wow' is this the future? If you go away by train then you have to pass it on the way in and if it's a night match and the lights are on, it still looks bright, shiny and new in design even now.

There are iconic grounds like Anfield, Elland Road, Stanford Bridge and Highbury. And also the special ones, grounds that are different from the norm like Craven Cottage, Southampton, Hartlepool. Football was a better place for it. I don't knock the new grounds; cleaner, safer with a great view from every seat. 'Seats', now there lays a can of worms – I'll talk more about them later. Thing is that the new grounds that have been built to replace the crumbling infrastructure of our football league are… well, all the same. I fail to see the difference between Darlington and the Riverside apart from location and size.

When you travelled away, it was apart of the adventure, the finding of each ground with its idiosyncrasies. Now they are built on the edge of a town with good access roads and proper sign posting from every motorway, making sure you can get to it safely and quickly and then escorted out again and on your way with little or no fuss. What fun is that? They look the same, they feel the same, they even sell the same food. You may as well be at home. There are a growing number of supporters up and down the land who seem to think that just letting them stand would bring back the atmosphere to our new flat packed soulless, corporate boxed grounds. But I'm not so sure, I believe a lot of people miss the push and shove, the not being able to see all of the pitch for most of the match, the smell of beer, sweat and farts drifting above the fans in great clouds of steam and cigarette smoke, just as much as anyone. I know I do but we have brought it upon ourselves that the game has become a more family-orientated spectator sport.

The picture I have in my mind of the perfect football ground is not a real one. It's the one in the painting by Mackenzie Thorpe called The Game. It shows row up on row of darkly lit street houses against a sky line of a great port with massive industrial works around it, right in the middle glowing bright is a football ground inviting you in. It could be any ground but it feels somehow northern and in the foreground is a small boy with a red football shirt, white shorts and red socks and a number 7 on his back. At first I used to think it was a young George Best. But now I'm more likely to think it's a representation of the small boy in all of us, looking on, wanting to join in and dreaming of one day playing there. We can all dream.

The 'other' Riverside.

Anonerimus

Doncaster v Middlesbrough,
Third Division, 9th May 1987
Score 0-2, Attendance 3,556

"We were at Doncaster an' it's raining. The home end is fully covered so we just pay on the gate an' walk into their home end no problem. We had a good cup of Oxo an' that. I'm looking round the ground thinking, oh yea proper old ground this, 'real' football, real supporters, even some flat caps then I'm looking more at the fans and the clothing they have on an' I'm just thinking how out of place we look when I see something strange. There's this local with a tiny terrier puppy tucked under his arm inside his jacket wrapped in a red, black an' white scarf.

I ask, "What the feck are ya doing wi that in here?"

The man looked puzzled and said, "Well a can't leave it in the car, it's only six weeks old."

I said, "Six weeks? Should it even be out of the house?"

"Oh, I'll get him a pie at half time, he'll be reet."

Man's best friend? **"**

Waiting in an... ticipation.

Anonerimus

Spurs v Middlesbrough,
Premier League, 26th October 2003
Score 0-0, Attendance 32,643

"We went to Spurs one year. We'd got some cheap tickets off a mate who worked for Sony so we are miles away from the Boro away fans. They were good seats an' all that in a neutral area but not quite hospitality. Not long before kick off, we notice that the block of about 20 seats just to the left of us is empty and has a few stewards keeping them free. Then just as the game gets under way, in comes all these young lads. We have to keep getting up to let them past. Now they don't say a word not even a "cheers mate" nothing, totally ignorant. My mate Lee has got no tact or manners at all and he's like, "Oh, ya all right, don't mind us, sorry for getting in ya way it's okay, you just stand on my toes that's fine."

As the game gets into full swing, these lads are up, out of their seat waving their arms around and stamping their feet. Then they start doing this thing that looked like they were all doing line dancing but in a Madonna vogue style. Still no noise but very off putting as we try to watch the match. Haha, I think I know what they are, so I turn to one of the stewards and ask him are they from the local deaf and dumb school? "Not all of them," he says, "some are just dumb". No sh*t, I think. But now the whole game is spoiled for us as we spend more time watching them, trying to work out what they are singing from the actions they make. By the second half I've had more than I can take and our mate Lee is huffing and puffing until he shouts over to the bloke in a high viz vest who looks like he's in charge, dead loud like, "Ow mate!! Can ya not get this lot to shut the feck up. I'm trying to watch the match here."

I just hung my head an' wanted to die. Now we know why he sold us the tickets cheap; we were in some sort of 'special needs' area an' thanks to Lee, we looked like we belonged.**"**

Anonerimus

Brighton HA v Middlesbrough,
Championship, 31st March 2012
Score 1-1, Attendance 20,553

❝Went to Brighton last season. Great weekend away, lovely atmosphere, nice new 'flat pack' ground. Whole day reminded me of when we first moved to the Riverside from Ayresome. The thing about that ground is the land around is owned privately so they can do what they want. The train drops you about 100 metres from the ground, nothing fancy, a bit like a metro station on the outskirts of Newcastle. You look at it and you think, yeah we could have had a train station as well. They also have no hot dog stands, no sweet vans, in fact no vendors at all. There is no pub just down the road either. So what you get is an enclosed ground that is the only type of amenity and that means it takes a fortune in beer and food sales.

They had the flag waving and the loud pig bag type of music to get the crowd going as well. At half time they rolled out the now obligatory new cheerleaders around the ground. Now up until this point the Boro fans had been on their best behaviour, no gay innuendo chants not even a "We can see you, we can see you holding hands". As the cheerleaders made their slow walk up to the away fans, these poor young lasses had on nothing but their little white hot pants and little blue crop tops. You could see the fear behind the false smiles and shaking pompoms. I braced myself for the normal, "Get ya t*ts out for the lads", but nothing came, only cheers and they danced their little hearts out. They finished with a cancan, high kick and the splits. At this point as the applause faded, one bloke just behind us about three rows from the front shouts at them, "Oi mate, ya c*ck's popped out!"

Oh well, never mind.**❞**

Anonerimus

Liverpool v Middlesbrough,
First Division, 5th November 1988
Score 3-0, Attendance 39,489

"In the late 80s I went on the coach to Liverpool with me dad and his mates from the club. I was well into it at the time, the clothes, everything. I can still remember what I had on that day, White Farha jeans, Patel blue La Coste polo shirt and a yellow Pringle jumper with my light brown loafers. They all took the piss with, "A ya going to a disco", an' all that.

I remember walking for an age down one long road to get to where we needed to be an' as we did, we stopped at a newsagent on a corner. I waited outside hanging around the ally next to it with loads of Boro pissing up a low wall. The police came over shouting something about pissin' up the side of the shop, but I was feeling cocky so I just pulled myself up backwards and sat on the wall. As soon as I did it, the police just stopped with stupid grins on their stupid faces. Then I smelt this funny smell and looked down at my hands. They had what looked like dog sh*t covering them. I jumped straight off the wall and my dad came out of the shop with his mates.

"What the f*ck have you been up to?" he started but the copper shouted over that he tried to warn us that the woman who owns the shop doesn't like people pissing up her shop on match day. And to stop them from sitting on her wall she put Brown Sauce on it.

When I looked round at my jeans, they were covered in the stuff and the back of me Pringle as well. I was gutted.

"Brown Sauce?" our dad's mate Ray said. "HP or Daddys?"

As they all laughed, our dad just said, "Come on sh*tty arse, you'll make us late for kick off.""

Anonerimus

Leeds v Middlesbrough,
Premier League, 30th March 1996
Score 0-1, Attendance 31,788

"My mate lost his keys on a trip to Elland Road some years back. After the match he asked a steward if he could radio in and see if they had been handed in.

"Can't miss 'em," he said. "They have a Boro Cars key ring on them."

So he did, and they had, an' my mate was told to go to the main ticket office to collect them. When he got them, every single one, even his car and house keys, had been bent at a 90 degrees angle. Dirty Yorkshire bastards. **"**

Blackburn v Middlesbrough,
Premier League, 25th October 2008
Score 1-1, Attendance 17,605

"The story I like is the one at Blackburn. We are getting beat 1-0 and at half time this lad comes out into the centre circle and asks their lass who's in the crowd to marry him over the PA system. And she goes, "Yes, but only if we beat Middlesbrough today." **"**

Anyone seen the burger van?

The voice of home... no matter what ground you're at.

Anonerimus

Brighton v Middlesbrough,
Championship, 31st March 2012
Score 1-1, Attendance 20,553

"Brighton two years ago was mint right from the moment we entered the place. My nephew Big Jon is sat in the back of the car goin', "He's gay… he's gay… he's defo gay him."

Then this cyclist passes us an' Jon goes, "He is sooooo gay."

I pipe up, "How, just how do ya know he's gay? Because he has Lycra on?"

Our Jon without looking says, "No… it's because he's taken the seat off his bike an' left 6" of pole sticking up."

Ya can't argue with the facts like. **"**

CHAPTER SEVEN: TEESSIDE AGGRO

Don't go out tonight unless ya red an' white...

I start this chapter with the statement that I do not wish to promote or glamorise violence at or around football matches in any way. That is why the number of stories from fans has been cut to just three from the many I was told or sent. I also hope they can show a different side to them and how you can unwillingly be caught up in the moment. I will leave the other stories for the growing number of true crime authors to write but I think anything new would be hard pushed to beat the book by Paul Debrick or John Theone. As a kid, I lived around the corner from Paul and he would pass you in the street unnoticed, but on a matchday it would have been a totally different story.

Let's face it, no set of supporters are angels. Middlesbrough have had their moments, both home and away over the years. From Ayresome Axeman to NTP, Block Two, Bob End Crew, BBC, SWC and Boro Boot Boys to the collective Front Line or the Redca' Casuals, the names make you want to laugh. These are tags of dishonour given by newspapers or urban myths told in pubs about extreme supporters held up to be admired. What is true is that every generation has its section of the crowd that are known to be more 'up for it' than others.

There have been times when, to be honest, I've been glad of the 20 to 30 or so lads who have rallied to the shouts of 'stand' when everyone around you is running away from on-rushing opposition supporters.

As an away supporter, you can easily slip into a false feeling of security cocooned in a ring of police protection. To the home supporter, it looks like the police are there to stop you getting at them as if we are dangerous creatures from a foreign land. But too easily the police can slip away to deal with other things leaving you at the mercy and good will of the home fans, as you drink their beer, abuse their home town reputation in song and try (mostly in vain) to defile their women. That's all it takes; two sets of fans singing rival songs, then an exchange of remarks and a flash point between just two people, then the whole world turns upside down. That's the reputation Boro away supporters had, not one of an organised planned military unit but one of an eagerness or willingness to join in en masse at the drop of a pint glass regardless of membership of the Front Line or not, as if it is inbred in our psyche, that old Teesside outsiders, 'backs against the wall' thing.

I think sometimes fans can be misunderstood, like our current gazette bad boys, The Red Faction. Each week they can be seen standing behind their banner reading 'Fans not Hooligans' but then they sing "Red moon on the rise", and do nothing to help their case. So what of the new young brand of supporters? I've drank in their pre-match pub, the Princess Alice, before the game many times like loads of supporters without even the suggestion of trouble. I've stood with them in the south east corner and thoroughly enjoyed every minute of it. I've also sat down and had a drink with them, talked to them about their image as 'ultras', a strange concept to most Boro fans who brand them as 'just kids'. Well, I have news for you, they are certainly not 'just kids', they are a group of serious, thought provoking younger men. They may well be the future of support at Middlesbrough FC. Who knows. This season could be the making of them now that they have in effect their own end. I may be wrong but labelling them as 'ultras' is about right, they are extreme supporters, flags, drums, flares (not six inch bell bottoms by the way) and god forbid singing at the match. Not only that but hold your breath… new songs. Football today and especially in the upper leagues is, as we all know, a world away from what it was. Clubs and supporters have moved on together. But the thing is, and here's the rub, as I said at the start of this chapter, that if the occasion was called upon and the shouts went up to 'stand' again, I believe that new and old supporters would not give an inch in true Boro style.

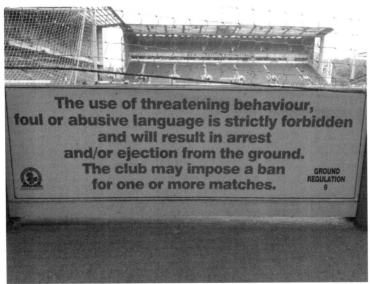

Right, that's the players… what about the fans?

The Lone Ranger and Tonto

We don't punch horses, do we?

Anonerimus

" I can't name the game or name any of the people who travelled, but this is the one that stands out in my mind. It's a good example of hooliganism for want of another name. It is vandalism and theft as well, all in one. What happened was that this ground had one of the portakabin-like kiosks. It sold Bovril, pies, crisps and all that. They closed the thing at the end of half time but I think they only put a wanky little padlock on the door. Now we had had a bit of trouble with the poor sods who worked it earlier and to be fair they did have attitude. As everyone poured out the back of the stand at the end of the game, the kiosk became a prime target. The door was kicked open and the hatch dropped down to reveal some 'known' faces inside beaming big fat smiles. "Right gentlemen, how can I help you?" They then started to hand out free food and cans to every fan who came past, hooligans or not. The problem was it was captured on camera an' then on the telly and in the papers the next day. Headlines and footage was all the same with "Boro fans run riot", that sort of thing.

But when I look back, all I remember is a bunch of lads away from home having a laugh and playing shops. No one got harmed but it did cost the home team a small fortune in Mars Bars and Coke. **"**

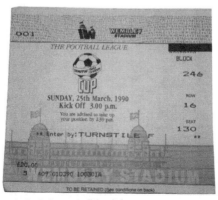

Bushwhacked on and off the pitch.

Anonerimus

Bristol Rovers v Middlesbrough,
Second Division, 20th April 1991
Score 2-0, Attendance 5,722

"We took the train down to Bristol. It's a long journey so plenty of time to drink on the way. Good banter and lots of singing as we get closer to Bristol itself. The train stopped at Temple Meads and on gets about 10 Brizzle supporters and two bobbys. A bit of friendly chanting between supporters is all that happens and we're soon into Bristol station. One of our lot has had way too much to drink on the way down so we're trying to keep him as far away from the view of the police as we can as we get off the train. I'm not sure how it happened but as we get onto the platform from the train, we find that we're trapped between the Bristol fans that got on at Temple Meads.

The police start pushing us forward, wanting us off the platform, but that's just forcing us into the Bristol supporters who are not moving, just milling around. A few things are said and a bit of pushing starts. At this point, the two bobbys who came with the Bristol fans from the train pile in on the first few Boro supporters. They have targeted our drunk mate who has been very loudly mouthing off at the Bristol lot. They grab him so we jump in and start to pull him away. As we do, one of the bobbys loses his balance and ends up on the floor. The other bobby then goes ballistic wading in with his stick just lashing out an' shouting for back up. Next thing, coppers are coming from all over. It's like they're popping up out of trap doors or something.

We grab our mate and push through the Bristol lads taking a few cuffs round the ear for our trouble but mostly unharmed. We are now running full pelt down the length of the station heading for the underpass and out into Bristol city centre. Our still drunk but no longer friend is still with us but obviously a lot slower. As we get to the bottom of the stairs and turn left to the exit he stops at the bottom, hands on knees saying he can't go on.

As I look back, he is sick all over the tiled floor. The police are coming down the stairs now and he lurches forward in a desperate attempt to get away, starting to run. The next time I look and as I turn to go up the stairs on the opposite side of the underpass, it's like a slow freeze frame from a silent movie. The first copper grabs our mate but slips on the sick on the floor. He's pulled along by our mate who is still trying to run and skids into the path of the second copper, knocking him into the wall. I stop in disbelief as all three crash to the floor with a big slap like sound. This must have held up anyone following because we got out and away. Two of us did get picked up about an hour later in a pub just opposite the station by the same coppers, coz we knew it was them by the smell of sick. **"**

No comment.

Anonerimus

Leeds v Middlesbrough, Second Division,
28th December 1989 • Score 2-1, Attendance 34,186

"The only time I've had any real trouble away was when I went to Leeds with my mate, Smart. He was a proper casual. He had all the gear and looked the biz like. The trouble started when the police tried to stop us near the ground.

There were about 100 of us being marched down from where the coaches had dropped us off. Now we had police at our backs pushing us on and police in front telling us to stop with a main road to our left and buildings to our right. We had no place to go, so Smart turns around to the coppers at the back and starts to have a go at them telling them to sort themselves out. Then a van pulls up an' out gets two dog handlers with their football supporters' best friends. We all look at this and just know it's going wrong. They are whipping these snarling barking dogs into a right frenzy. A bus into town trundles past and stops on the other side of the road. Two or three lads make a break for it and run across the road to get on the bus, then another two, then we all just leg it. I jump on okay but Smart gets pulled back. He's got this great snarling German Sheppard hanging off his arse, teeth ripping his jeans. One last effort and he's on, shouting abuse at the police as the bus pulls away. Smart is bleating about his bum bleeding an' it's all wet. When I have a look, it's covered in slaver but the only thing the dog has ripped into is his jeans and he's missing the arse pocket on the right hand side. It was all waste of time anyway. They stopped the bus at the next stop and we all had to get off. After the match, we're being marched away back to our coaches when Smart spots the same dog handler and his nuttier dog.

"Stay here," he says and walks over to the copper. I can't hear what he's saying but after a second or two, the copper goes to the front of the van and comes back with Smart's f*cking back pocket. Amazing. Smart says, "These cost me a fortune these."

If ya don't ask, ya don't get'.**"**

68

CHAPTER EIGHT: LOCAL DERBIES

The cock of the north...

How many times have you been told by Newcastle or Sunderland supporters that "It's not a proper derby" or "You're nothing to us, it's just another three points"? We let them say what they want when it's all they can say. Yes, they are bigger clubs, larger fan base, bigger stadiums, higher turnover and, yes, in their history both clubs have won loads more trophies and titles than us. This, Boro fans can't and never dispute.

But show me a Sunderland or Newcastle supporter under the age of 40 and I'll show you someone who has never seen his team lift a cup in his lifetime and that's so sad. Is bigger better? Not from our side of the fence. We will always be the underdogs and that's great. They may have all the bark but we have always had the bite.

I have a friend who's from Newcastle and he would love to see the Boro in the Premier League again and not just for the six points they would take off us. But he truly believes that all the north east clubs should be represented. He wants the atmosphere that only a non-derby derby game can bring. He once said that when he's watching Middlesbrough v Sunderland, he cheers us on like we were the Toon. Really? But I must say I'm the same; when Newcastle play Sunderland at the Stadium of Sh*te, I'm rooting for the Toon. Actually, I'm rooting for the stand to collapse and then spontaneously burst into flames as the pitch opens up and the devil claims them back to whatever hell they originally came from.

The main difference for me between Geordies and Mackems is their attitude to other football teams. When I lived in Newcastle, I found you could actually have a real conversation about football with most Geordies. They are, as a rule, knowledgeable about other teams and the history of the game in general. They are also interested in what you think of them and their team. Not that they don't take the piss because they do and are quick to point out our club's failings in a very astute way. But Mackems are a completely different animal. They look at football from one point of view. That is that all other teams are sh*t. They seem to have this almost blind conviction regardless of any actual facts. They are also so aggressive towards other teams. A Geordie will mock you and tease you about your club. A Mackem will just be offensive and angry for no other reason than you're not a Sunderland supporter. Don't get me wrong, Newcastle supporters can be right nasty bastards when they want and no more so to Sunderland fans. But I think from my own experience, Sunderland supporters truly 'hate' Newcastle while Newcastle fans tend to just laugh at Sunderland supporters revelling in how wound up they can get them.

Saying all that, Newcastle fans can be a bit funny too. My wife worked for Northern Electric in Newcastle and in her office there were two middle aged blokes, one Sunderland and one Newcastle fan. They had been lifelong friends and then when Sunderland started to build the Stadium of Sh*te, just for a laugh he bought his mate a present for his birthday. He opened it at work and there was a framed certificate to say that he was the proud owner of a commemorative Sunderland supporter's brick with his name on and that it was going into building the new ground. To say he was not happy would be an understatement. They had known each other for over 20 years and from that day they never spoke again.

Top Trumps anyone?

Anonerimus

Sunderland v Middlesbrough,
FA Cup, 29th January 2012
Score 1-1 (3-2 on agg), Attendance 33,275

"A friend of mine who supports Darlington is so unfortunate that he is forced by his company to work in Sunderland city centre (why we are made to call it a 'city' when we all know it's just a large car park and shopping centre with the stench of urine hanging over it is beyond me).

Every morning on his way to work and every evening on his way back, he has to cross the Wearmouth bridge to Monkwearmouth where he parks his car. Every day, he passes the same sign on both sides. It reads: 'In DESPAIR, contact SAMARITANS, 08457909090, supported by the local NHS'.

Now, he looks at this as a warning for anyone entering Sunderland for the first time and then again as counselling for them as they leave after the trauma of their visit. But I look at this way: to get to and from the Stadium of Sh*te, the home supporters have to cross the self same bridge. How bad must it be to be a Sunderland supporter that the local NHS sponsors suicide notices for people going to and then from their home games. **"**

IN DESPAIR

CONTACT
SAMARITANS

08457 909090

Supported by the local N.H.S.

Anonerimus

Newcastle v Middlesbrough,
First Division, 1st February 1975
Score 2-1, Attendance 42,514

" Every time we talk about Newcastle, my dad always tells this story about when they went up in the 70s. The story he tells is that they had one or two drinks around the Hay Market and then wandered into Fenwick's with about an hour to go before kick off. As they are looking around at the suits, he sees Frank Spraggon.

"Aw do Frank," he says (like he knew him). "Only an hour to go, ya know."

Then Frank apparently says his wife was taking back Christmas presents and he's lost her in the shop somewhere. Me dad then says he asked a shop girl to put an announcement out for a Mr Spraggon's wife to come to customer service as the match kicks off in an hour and the Boro would be without one of their best players. But they never did. He reckons it was deliberate to try and scupper our chances. **"**

Have you ever seen a Mackem lift a cup?

Anonerimus

Sunderland v Middlesbrough,
First Division, 21st March 1995
Score 0-1, Attendance 16,501

"We went to the 'old Joker Park' a long time ago now to see probably one of the worst Boro sides ever. The match was a total goalless bore draw. The only thing that kept it interesting was the banter between the fans.

In central midfield that day was a young Jamie Pollock who, after taking one too many late tackles at the start of the match, started to put himself about a bit. I remember him launching himself into a tackle on the halfway line that he should never have won and the ball spinning clear then getting up and then jumping in on the loose ball as two Sunderland players ran to collect it. Again he emerged with the ball, knocking them on their arses before off loading it. Great cheers from the Boro fans with a rousing chorus of "One Jamie Pollock" followed by a "Jamie Pollock ugly bast*rd" from the Sunderland fans. Then again an' again they kept on singing it. Ya can't blame them they had found a song to sing and the game was crap so why not indulge in a bit of 'mock the afflicted'.

This continued for just about all of the second half with the odd shout of "Esmeralda" and "the bells, the bells" an' then… something quite wonderful happened. From a throw in on the right hand side, as we watched from behind the Sunderland goal, the ball broke to a green shirt who pumped it forward high between the two Mackem centre backs and who should be racing through but the very same 'ugly basterdos' who then took an age to control the ball as he entered the penalty box with the two centre backs and the goal keeper closing in on him. The ball then looked to hit a divot or get a touch from a defender just as the keeper was about to take the three oncoming players out in one go. It bounced up, hit Pollock on the knee and bobbed slowly into the left hand corner (some stories say it hit him in the face). He then ran to the away fans like Berine scoring a hat trick. Well, the rest of the game was played out with the full Boro support singing at the top of their voice, "Jamie Pollock, ugly bast*rd , Jamie Pollock ugly bast*rd." Great engine, with little natural talent, but with a big, big heart.**"**

Not a day for the faint-hearted.

Anonerimus

Sunderland v Charlton,
Premier League, 13th August 2005
Score 1-3, Attendance 34,446

"I was in Sunderland for a wedding once (can I just say it was none of my family). We had a few sherbets on the afternoon before the main event in the 'glass factory'. Sounds funny but it was actually a great venue. We met up with some other friends from all round the country and mooched from bar to bar wasting time. We knew Sunderland were at home but as the wedding was at about 2pm we thought we would miss most of the supporters. This was true until we walked into this Yates and found ourselves in the middle of a pre-match Open Mic question and answer session with an ex-Sunderland player. We're all suited and booted and we got a few looks but nothing much. It's actually very interesting listening to other sets of fans complain and worry about the same things we do.

Time moved very slowly; most of us have finished our drinks and are just standing up to leave, when the compere who must have been bored as well with the same old questions, shouts over to us, "You're looking very smart today, ladies and gentlemen, would any of you like to ask a question before you go?"

We say, "No thanks, we're just off now."

But then 'The Boy' Wade pipes up, "Aye I've got one for ya."

The mic is handed over and he says, "After last season and all things considered, looking to the future, can you just tell me why Sunderland are so f*cking sh*te?"

At first no one has twigged that he's from Newcastle and the ex-pro starts to try and answer the question. As he starts talking, Wade just walks out of the pub and we all follow, bursting with laughter. When we get outside, we start to do a little jog an' duck into what is possibly the worst shopping centre in the history of retail.**"**

Anonerimus

Newcastle v Middlesbrough,
Championship, 20th December 2009
Score 2-0, Attendance 49,644

"I have a friend who is a Newcastle supporter but lives in the Boro and the company he works for got me and three mates free tickets to Newcastle v Middlesbrough. We went up and met him and a few of his mates before the match for a friendly drink. We must have went to about four pubs and are getting on great with these lads. We stopped at a pub next to the Grainger Market that had a band singing a mix of toon chants and 60's tunes, getting everyone going. The band asks for any requests so two of us go off for a piss leaving our mate with the rest of the Newcastle crowd. Unknown to us as we go, one of our newfound friends asks the bloke to sing a song for our mate as he's a Boro supporter and probably feeling left out. When we come out, the place is ringing to the sound of Fog on the Tyne which it goes like this, "Fog on the Tyne is all mine all mine, fog on the Tyne's all mine" then they all start pointing at our mate singing, "Sh*t on the Tees is all hee's all hee's, sh*t on the Tees is all hee's."

I don't even think we finished our pint. **"**

Anonerimus

Newcastle v Middlesbrough,
Second Division, 17th March 1984
Score 3-1, Attendance 30,421

"When I was a little girl, my dad would take me to see Middlesbrough most weeks. He even got me a little fold-out stool to stand on. I would stand at the right hand bottom corner of the Holgate on my stool just so when the players came to take a corner I could see them right up close. I remember one time putting hands through the railings stretching out until it hurt my arm just to touch George Best.

But then when I got older I started courting my husband and Saturdays were his only day off, so I stopped going as my husband was not a football fan at all. Years later on one of our anniversaries as a surprise he took me to see Newcastle v Middlesbrough at St James' Park. He knew that I'd always wanted to go and my dad had always said we would but never got the chance. We had a lovely meal and then took our places for the game where we had 'posh seats' as my dad would say.

After the game we went into the lounge for a drink and it was all very nice. Then a group of men behind us started getting quite loud, one in particular a big bald man with a strong Newcastle accent was f'ing and blinding and really being very derogatory about the Middlesbrough players. This went on for some time and they started to get louder. In the end I turned and said to this chap that I did not like his language and that I was a Middlesbrough supporter and that he was spoiling a lovely day on my anniversary. Well, his face dropped and he became very apologetic and insisted on buying me and my husband a drink. As he went off to sort them out, my husband said, "I may not like football and I may not know any of our team, but even I know who Jack Charlton is." Well, when he came back with the drinks, I practically did a curtsy. Thankfully my husband led me away before I embarrassed him anymore. **"**

CHAPTER NINE: WEMBLEY

Tell ya Mam, ya Mam, t'put the champagne on ice...

Do you remember when there was a time when going to Wembley was destined never to be? In fact, one of our greatest songs ever sang is about not going and not winning, such was our resignation that it would never happen.

But then that miracle happened and not for the last time in our history. We somehow managed to get ourselves into the final of the doomed idea that was the Zenith Data Cup and again not for the last time against the might of Chelsea. We all went down in our tens of thousands for our first taste of Wembley Wonder. I think the first time at Wembley for some was probably their first time in London as well. That's how mad football can make you. Why would you go to London if not for the football or maybe Legoland Windsor at a push. It was like a mythical place and so the first time we don't really see how crap it was. That the toilets didn't work, that the stewards only just spoke English, that the PA system was inaudible and the food inedible, that Chelsea gave us a kicking outside the ground and on the pitch, sending us on our way like the Northern small town gate crashers we were. But you know what, we loved it. And we wanted more.

If the Zenith Data Cup final was a bit of a fluke, then the League Cup against Leicester was just reward for all the hard work that had gone into the club during the years in between. It was, as we all know, total heartbreak and at the hands of a man schooled by one of our own. We all know we out-played them, we all know it was ours to take home. But as every Boro fan knows, that's not the Boro way. With one hand on the cup and us lot all singing of victory, someone forgot to tell Martin O'Neill. From where we were sat, we could see him running up and down shouting instructions. Every throw-in on that side, every break in play, he was shouting, shouting at them. I remember my brother saying, "I wish he would shut up and sit down." He never did and we all went home broken.

I'm not sure why but that result is a little bit of what makes it special to be a Middlesbrough FC supporter. That's because I've never been so proud of being a Boro fan as that day. After the final whistle, the volume and the emotion when we sang defiantly over and over again, "We shall overcome", was spine-tingling.

I think we can all agree these were heady times to be an away supporter for the Boro. The Premier League grounds every week, massive support, high profile players and fast-breaking counter-attacking football away from home. I genuinely beloved that we had a chance of winning every game we played.

Then Chelsea again. It was a like a dream. The thing I remember most was the feeling of wonder on that day. Fans you talked to on the tube seemed more up for it, as if this was the 'big one' and everything before had been a rehearsal. Forget the league, this is the one we wanted. That was the atmosphere outside and in the ground there was one of defiant optimism. Most people I have talked to actually believed we would win that day. It all came together as one massive pre-kick off protest about the deduction by the FA of those three little points. Just how good was it as a supporter to actually voice your disgust on live TV against the FA officials now being introduced to the teams? When I talked to a Chelsea fan after the game, despite the fact that we were all chanting, "Three points… three points", he said, "What was that fascist salute thing all about?" Oh well, it was the best part of the whole day for me. But then again, was it just another crazy day supporting Boro back in them times of disbelief?

The thing is, away supporters talk now about them years as some of the best. To go ground to ground wondering what Boro side would turn up. Would we match the big teams blow for blow or would we be turned over by smaller clubs with less ambition scrabbling for points and who would eventually finish above us in the table?

A lot of water had passed under the Transporter in a very short space of time when the League Cup came round again. From the little I remember and from what my friends tell me, there was an awful lot more general drunkenness and aggression this time round. But we all again made the long expensive journey 'darn sarf'. It was like a chore… "Oh no love, I've got to go to Wembley again. What a bummer. I'll be back in two days skint and depressed as usual, ba-bye now."

And so the feeling of inevitability settled in nicely as we once again capitulated to the sound of Chelsea singing, "Can we play you every year", or "2-nil, we always win 2-nil". I remember stopping off in Northampton for the night on the way back, having to get leathered and giving the locals some chew. It was for the best when I think about it. Families of away supporters must have dreaded the thought of dad coming home yet again wanting to smash the house up like a scene from Ripping Yarns Golden Gordon and the flip side is the last thing you want to hear when you get home, "But did ya have a nice time though?"

We shall overcome somedayyyyyyyyyy...

Anonerimus

Chelsea v Middlesbrough,
Zenith Data Cup Final, 25th March 1990
Score 1-0, Attendance 76,369

❝ Where I worked in Eston, there was this butcher called Dave and he was a right one. When Middlesbrough got through to the Zenith Data Cup final way back in 1990, tickets were like rocking horse sh%ot. Davey, who had a ticket, would ask people if they were going and inevitably some would say they couldn't get a ticket. Dave would say, 'Oh, do ya know where I got mine from? McKenzie's decorators in South Bank," telling them that he'd been doing coaches for away games on the side and from Monday morning he would be doing a coach and a ticket for £50 but you had to be there early.

Come Monday morning there was a line of about 70 people snaking its way past the old Yorkshire bank to the front door of McKenzie's. People went nuts and their phone never stopped. 'Course they had no tickets.

When people came back to Davey, he said, "I know, the robbin' bastard had £20 deposit off me an' I've not had it back yet." He was some boy, I tell ya. ❞

Anonerimus

Chelsea v Middlesbrough,
Zenith Data Cup Final, 25th March 1990
Score 1-0, Attendance 76,369

"I was very young when we went to Wembley for the first time. I really wanted to go but my dad was on 2 'til 10 or a 6 'til 2 or whatever it was called at ICI Wilton and no one would swop shift with him. So my Uncle Jon said he would take me an' could get tickets no problem. This was great as I looked up to my Uncle Jon and we would have a great fun day out.

The train down really was great fun. We got pies and crisps from the trolley an' I thought that was mint being about 11 at the time an' never having been any further than Newcastle or York. The songs and the blokes all having a drink an' that was an amazing thing for a young lad.

But everything changed as we neared London and everyone started to get ready to get off. Our Uncle Jon got all serious and sat me down.

"I've promised ya dad I'd look after ya so I need ya to be on ya best okay? Stick with me all the time. Ya can even hold me hand if ya want when we get into a crowd, all right mate?"

By the time we had left the train and got to the front entrance of King's Cross, I had to look out for pickpockets, foreigners, paedophiles, bag snatchers (we didn't even have a bag), con men, funny food, knife gangs, Millwall supporters and he may even have mentioned the Kray twins at some point.

Then I had a list of things I shouldn't do: look people in the eye, talk to anyone who was not a confirmed Middlesbrough supporter, drink any water from a tap and lastly go to the toilet on my own.

We got lucky and fell in with a family with two kids from the Boro. This meant that according to Jon the "Total mystery of the tube map" would be okay as we would just follow all the other Boro supporters. By some miracle it actually worked. I had a great time at the match and to be honest couldn't have give a toss about the result. I thought the whole thing was great and still do. All day Jon had been leading me round with supreme confidence, pointing out landmarks and information all about the wonders of our great capital city while keeping a ninja-like eye out for danger.

After the match, he was like a man on a mission and we practically ran from tube to tube until we got back to King's Cross and jumped on the train home. I think we made it with about half an hour to spare. When we sat down, I could see him physically shrink into his chair with relief.

We had a good laugh on the way back about what we had seen an' done that day; he even made me a beer shandy with the drinks he got from the buffet car. When we got to Darlo we phoned me mam, and my dad came to give us a lift home. From the conversation in the car, I realised that my Uncle Jon had in fact never been to London before an' everything he told me was just what he'd read or seen on TV. But I never said owt to me dad and I never thought of him as a bullsh*tter; it just made me love him more to think that he would do that for me. He never had kids but I think he would have made a great dad.**"**

Ticket to a whole world of pain.

Anonerimus

"The Zenith Data final was a very very long day going down on the coach, all the way from The Bankers ground to Wembley.

But I always remember the Turners (Painting and Decorators) lads singing the best songs. They sang "Champion the wonder horse" and the classic "Bom bom, dee bom, debom, debom… bom bom, dee bom, debom… debom… bom… bom… barubadumbom… Wow tie a yellow ribbon round the old Oak Leaf. It's been three long years…" I am smiling right now thinking of it. (The Oak Leaf was a ruff as club in the centre of Southbank).**"**

"For the Leicester game at Wembley, we amassed at the Torch just off Wembley Way. Some Leicester fans were kicking a ball from one side of the car park back to the other. Each kick was followed by a "OOOoooo sh*t ahhhhh", then one went a bit a stray and landed in our lot.

Our Mac took up the ball and volleyed it right over the top of the pub and into some gardens shouting, "Right now f*ck off and go play up ya own end", followed by, "Don't you look at me like that, I know who ya mam is." **"**

The twin towers of disappointment.

Anonerimus

Chelsea v Middlesbrough,
FA Cup Final, 17th May 1997
Score 2-0, Attendance 79,160

"We got into a massive crush at the exit to Wembley tube and the police told us to stop while they halted the traffic outside. So we are all crushed together, Boro and Chelsea, but one Chelsea fan stood about 3 foot above everyone. It's gone all quiet like we're all in a lift or something. Then this Boro fan leans over another and pulls at this man mountain's shirt, rubbing it between his fingers as he goes in a very camp voice, "OOooo is that silk? I bet it is an' such a lovely colour, sets ya eyes off a treeet."

The Mountain just looks down on him as we all snigger. This lad obviously can't help himself so he now leans right over and loudly sniffs at the Blue Hulk. Then turning and shouting in again a very camp voice to no one in particular, "Ahhh Paco Rabanne, everyone, I told you, Paco Rabanne."

I'm not sure why but for some reason all the Boro fans cheered like we knew all about it and then the police let us go. And the big fella still never said a word.**"**

CHAPTER TEN: CARDIFF

We shall overcome...

Middlesbrough v Bolton,
Carling Cup Final 2004
Score 2-1, Attendance 72,634

People said it just felt different, no pressure, just going down for the day out and all the other things we tell ourselves to offset the pain of impending disappointment. I agree our own plan was to just go down, get pissed and enjoy the day without even getting a ticket. Maybe watch it in a pub.

Then things slowly started dropping into place. My niece was at uni in Cardiff so we could meet up with the locals for a drink. The four other members of the family who had missed the last couple of Wembleys had got tickets so they were coming down. To top it all, my cousin who lived in London had blagged a press pass off her mate who worked for the Irish Times and told her, "The last thing I want to do is spoil a good day off by going to watch Middlesbrough v Bolton in Wales." You can see his point. But she was in like Flynn. Other things happened around the build up, 'omens' if you will. Supporters south had a big meeting the night before in Swindon, exactly where we planned to meet up and sleep at an old mate's house. Then a couple of apparently top tickets were offered to us at face value. This was all going far too well.

We had left it very late to try an' get some place to stay in Cardiff itself, so I called the branch of Cardiff YHA as a last resort and they said we could join on the day we arrived... cost for a six month membership plus B&B? £12.50 Ker'ching! God was obviously smiling on us and he never stopped. My personal favourite memory (and there are many) was not my hugging of Steve Gibson outside of Wetherspoon's (this will, however, stay with me for life), but seeing one of Joseph Job's relations who had travelled over for the match in floods of tears just inside the stairwell and every Boro fan to a man walking up to him and giving him a hug or a pat on the back.

We 'overcame' and it was strange. I remember coming out of the ground and asking our kid, "Right, what do we do now?" having never been in the position of winning. It felt alien.

"Oh, we conquer Europe now, kidder," he said.

If only.

Rock the bus, E-I-O!

Anonerimus

"On the way down to Cardiff, our kid tells the younger lads in our group that, "All Welsh lasses take it from behind in bus shelters".

They're all goin', "Really Baz, how do you know that like?"

He has their attention now. "Well, I know from an actual opinion poll carried out in 1999 when I was stationed there... It's a fact."

"What opinion poll was that?"

He's beaming now. "In my opinion," he says laughing, "coz the only two I got off with did, haha!"

I'm not even sure why he was laughing. The sh*t you say to pass the time when you're away from home. **"**

·

"First pub we went into in Cardiff after the match was called the Queens (not a gay bar by the way). It was a fantastic pub, all wood and brass. The staff could not have been any better and really joined in with the occasion.

As we go in, it's not yet packed and there's this bloke just been served at the bar, fresh pint in hand. We stand next to him waiting to be served. He lifts up his pint and takes a long slow pull on it, draining down to about half way in one go.

"What's the lager taste like?" I ask him.

He holds it up to the light and then makes a tutting sound. "Ta... ta... ta... tastes like errrrr success, mate. F*cking success. A like it, a might even have some more." Then he turns and looks at us with a big smile on his face.

We all have a little laugh.

The barman comes and asks us what he can get us.

"Two pints of f*cking success, mate, please," I say an' we all laugh a little bit louder. That pub and that night will stay with me for a very long time. **"**

Anonerimus

"A sang all night in the pubs around Cardiff city centre fuelled by beer with whisky and ginger chasers until eventually my throat gave out. Do you know what? I really can't remember seeing a single Bolton fan all night.

The last pub we're in, we get talking to some good lads from Pally Park. The atmosphere was great and they start off sing a few chants. I'm obviously taking a rest as my throat is in bits and I'm feeling a bit 'fally over' after all the whisky. One of them says I'm a bit quiet and to give them a song to lead them off like. The first thing that comes into my head is this song to the tune of 'He's got the whole world in his hands'.

"A got a German Sheppard dog named Prince,
A got a German Sheppard dog named Prince,
A got a German Sheppard dog named Prince,
Because me one called Sheba died."

Total stone wall looks from everyone around me. I must have looked a right dick. But did I give a feck? We had just won our first domestic cup and if I remember Newcastle had been beaten that day by one goal from a player they sent on loan to another club. Never got much better than that. **"**

Err what do we do now?

Dreams do come true.

Anonerimus

"After the final in Cardiff, we found this row of chippys and take aways. This local lad we had been talking to sent us to a chip shop right at the end of the street. He told us to get the special with sauce. The first two just got chips or something but I thought no, why not and asked for a special with sauce. Well, this big fat old woman pulled out what I thought was a large battered sausage, then picked up what I thought was the brown sauce and covered it without asking how much I wanted. It wasn't 'til I got it outside an' I smelled it that I realised it was sweet. What I'd got was a battered banana with chocolate sauce and it was a taste sensation. It had a sweet pancake/doughnut-like batter. It was bloody lovely. I think the old boiler must have took a shine to us coz when the lads went in and asked for one, she said she would batter their bananas any time. All the women are well dirty in Cardiff by the way. "

CHAPTER ELEVEN: EINDHOVEN

Small town in Europe, just a...

All the rollercoasters in 'mingoland' could not have prepared us for this. When doctors try to explain out of body experiences, they should just say, "You know, like when Middlesbrough were in a European cup final? Well, that's what it's like."

That's just what other teams around the country must have thought. Like watching someone you know on telly, it's them, but it doesn't seem real. The consensus of opinion was that Steve McClaren was in fact a bit of a genius on the quiet, or that we had stumbled upon a group of players who actually gave a sh*t. A friend of mine who had been to a lot of away games during our first wander through Europe's back waters said, 'They're all crap. None of 'em would last a season in the Prem." If he could see it then surely the players who played in them games must have felt it too because it stood them in good stead for what was about to happen next.

Second time around, we walked the historical city streets of the place known now simply as 'Europe' and we walked with a swagger. This band of away supporters became very specialist, almost elite. The day trippers or one time wonders made up the bulk of those away days but some made nearly every game. I personally didn't bother (I use the word 'bother' because although it would have been hard, if I really wanted to, I could have done and to my shame I didn't think it was worth it, how wrong was I?) but others did, some to great personal sacrifice. They racked up a collection of ticket stubs I would die for.

Imagine sat at the BBC Sports Personality of the Year event with Alan Hanson on your table: Scottish First Division, Football League First Division x 8, FA Cup x 2, League Cup x 4, Super Cup, FA Charity Shield x 6, oh and European Cup x 3 all winning medals. All very nice, Alan, but check this out (as you slip the ticket from your wallet): Boro v Steaua Bucharest... home and away! Boro fan 1 – Smug Jock Twat nil, I think you'll find.

Before we move on, I think it would be wrong not to talk about the trouble we encountered on our travels. But out of respect for the supporters who suffered, I thought it would be good to include a short extract from a British police official report as reported by the Daily Mail. This is not to glorify what happened and I'm sure you will have noticed, I avoided it in a previous chapter just for that reason.

Daily Mail 16th March 2006

Middlesbrough fans who braved a hostile trip to Rome have earned praise for their behaviour.

They had been urged not to cause trouble at last night's UEFA Cup match after three Boro supporters were stabbed during an ambush by Italian hooligans the night before.

They kept their cool in the face of a series of confrontations, a senior British police officer who was in Rome to cover the game said.

Despite having to wait in the ground for almost two hours after the match finished 2-1 to Roma – an aggregate of 2-2 meaning Boro went through on away goals – fans did not get too frustrated. Supt Steve Swales said, 'I left the stadium after an hour and found the streets back to the city were deserted.

'The fans were held back for one hour 40 minutes and by the time they found their coaches, it was almost two hours before they left.

'However, I would like to praise the supporters for their behaviour during this 'hold-back' period.

'While they were no doubt frustrated, they were good-natured.

'They sang and chanted and did not let their feelings boil over.'

After talking to many dedicated away fans, it's obvious that this was total blind faith, the kind of unquestioning support that borders on only one thing: LOVE. I know, "We love you, Boro, we do", but it wasn't until this campaign that it became obvious to me that there are some away supporters who just love it more than others. To these elite few, if you are reading this, you have my total respect. You are indeed Golden Gods. But in the same measure I think you are all totally Barmy Army.

If you put to one side the emotion of the semi final, the injustice of the ticket allocation and the disappointment of the actual result, once all romance and anger are stripped away, what we're left with is an incredible achievement. A true force of will by a club, its players and most of all, their supporters. From most people who went, I got a feeling of sadness but not disappointment. The key is in the song, our anthem that was taken with us and sang home an' away. It's derogatory and defiant in the same breath. Probably the cleverest chant we have ever sung. "Small town in Europe, we're just a small town in Europe." Pure Boro through and through.

But it was best summed up by a much more eloquent man than me (of which there are many). He knew nothing about us before that season yet he captured what we hoped everyone could see.

"You have the satisfaction of knowing that, although your team did not win the game, your supporters present in Eindhoven proved to the world that football fans can turn a match into a friendly, violence-free celebration."
UEFA Chief Executive Lars-Christer Olsson

Now when I started this, I asked why people follow Boro away. What do they get out of it and what do they say about our town that they unwittingly represent on their travels? Well, do you know what, Lars ya daft old bugger? What you said there, that'll do nicely my mate.

Song anyone?

"Jingle bells, jingle bells, jingle all the way, oh what fun it is to see the Boro lose away, Oy!"

*From Wembley to Europe,
we follow... follow... follow...*

Anonerimus

*Sporting Lisboa v Middlesbrough,
UEFA Cup, 17th March 2005
Score 1-0, Attendance 21,217*

"Sat in this bar in Portugal talking to this German fella, who spoke such good English it was embarrassing, I'm telling him how it was an adventure following Boro round Europe . He was amazed that I have never been to some of these countries before having been to nearly every country in Europe himself. So I told him me dad in his first job had drove all round Europe when he was younger.

"Oh, lorry driver, drive round, stop and deliver?" he said in almost perfect English.

"No, mate, he was in the Army, Armoured Division, he used to drive round, stop and kill people… Boom! Boom!"

Eeeeeerrrrr either he had no sense of humour or he didn't like Basil Brush. I don't know? Anyway the old ones are the best.**"**

Sevilla fans gave us daft saucer hats but they kept the cup.

Anonerimus

AS Roma v Middlesbrough,
UEFA Cup, 15th March 2006
Score 2-1 (2-2 on agg, Boro through on away goal),
Attendance 32,642

"Our mate was right looking forward to going to Roma and we're all sat in the Clevo talking about it. He goes, "Am looking forward to going to the take aways me like."

We stop and look at him an' ask why?

"A just can't wait me. A bet the Parmos are f*ckin' massive."

We tell him that they probably don't do any out there.

"What?" he says. "Ya jokin' arn' ya? All the Italians round here do 'em."

We had to carefully explain to him it was invented here on Teesside. He was so upset he got a right hump on. For all these years he thought he was being dead cosmopolitan. He doesn't even eat curry an' chips!

Then we started on who invented it. Was it some place in Stockton or was it the Europa in town? Still I'm pretty sure it wasn't some place in Rome.**"**

What was that ticket allocation again?

Anonerimus

Sevilla v Middlesbrough,
UEFA Cup Final, 10th May 2006
Score 4-0, Attendance 36,500

"Not so long ago I was in the Nops club having a swift pre-match pint or two. I was talking about this book when someone leans over and says, "I've got a story for your book, if ya really want to know what supporting the Boro is all about?"

I was happily shown a wall of Boro supporters' photos home and away, visiting away supporters and Boro supporters from all over the world coming to watch Middlesbrough play. Each photo has a little message or description underneath so you know who it is. In lots of these photos was a diminutive figure stood right at the front of most of the group pics. She was an older lady, decked out in full colours, smiling proudly and obviously enjoying herself being right in the middle of everyone. "That's me mam," she says, "she's the one I want to tell you about."

As it happens, she's a bit of a celebrity in the Nops and while I'm there, lots of people ask, "Where's ya mam?" or "Is little legs not going today?" Although I'm not going to mention her name, I think most people will know her anyway just from what I've said. Turns out she's in her late seventies and has been a Boro supporter all her life, season ticket holder, and supporters club, the works. She follows the Boro home and away, rain or shine, total dedication; the sort of supporter that genuinely makes you feel proud.

The year of our Eindhoven adventure she never missed a European game travelling and supporting the Boro everywhere they went, no matter how far or at what personal cost. Imagine then, the thrill she had at the end of that long long traumatising emotional ride when Massimo finally headed in 'that goal'.

But wait. As everyone knows there was a twist at the end, a new way for the club to add to the stress of actually qualifying and that was the ticket allocation lotto. So no matter how devoted she had been, no matter how much she had shown her loyal support all over Europe, she now found herself ticketless for potentially the biggest game in the club's history. This disappointment was only made worse by people she knew who had never been to any of the European home games, let alone the away games, coming up to her, telling her they had tickets and basically laughing.

Now this is where this lady differs from most. Sure she was upset and maybe just a little bit angry. But she was still determined that the club she had loved for all this time would not stop her from supporting them in their biggest game. So with the help of her son, his wife and their eldest daughter, she got a lift down to Hull and got herself onto a ferry bound for the final leaving the car behind. On board and it's packed with Boro supporters, all singing, having a great time and in no time is up leading them in a rendition of "Peter Reid's got a f****n monkey's heed!!"

At the ground, she meets old friends and family just out of the blue. All of them can't believe she has no ticket but are glad she's made it. As with everyone that day, singing and drinking and a great time was had. She was a great hit with all the Seville fans and locals alike. As most of the fans drifted off to the game, her son's eldest daughter stayed with her in a bar they'd found who supplied them with free pizza as they watched the game unfold.

After the game, they stayed over in Holland for the night then took the ferry back to Hull. When they got back to the car, some student friends had brick-walled the car into its parking space with the message 4-0 written on it.

I asked if it had been a disappointment for her but was told, "No, she loved it, seeing all them people, meeting all them away fans and supporting the Boro. She was in her element!"

Now that's what being an away supporter or just a supporter is all about: unconditional love for your team. The club may not always show they love you back, but that's not the point of real support. When you think of all them photos on the wall, of all them different supporters, I just wonder if there's a bar in Spain just the same and if there's a photo of a lady Boro supporter with the caption 'Boro Poco Piernas'. I'd like to think so and so should you. **"**

The great Anon-erimus.